*To Leonard
with love in Yeshua*

# Provision

## Signs, Wonders, and Miracles
## in the Life and *Aliyah* of a Messianic Jew

*I thought it good to declare the signs and wonders that the
Most High God has worked for me. How great are His signs,
and how mighty His wonders! His kingdom is an everlasting kingdom, and His dominion is from generation to generation.* (Dan 4:2-3)

**Raymond Robert Fischer**

Olim Publications
P.O. Box 2111, Tiberias, Israel
E-mail: Olim@kinneret.co.il

Design: David Coddington-Studio Mapal-Israel

Copyright © 2001 by Raymond R. Fischer
P.O. Box 2111, Tiberias, Israel

**ISBN 965-90397-0-0**

**Printed in Israel**

To the Lord God of Israel: the God of Abraham, Isaac, and Jacob, the Great Provider of everything.

And to, my three darling daughters, Robin Michele Fischer Kraak, Cynthia Carole Fischer and Julie Alice Fischer Froke who, after Himself and Donna, their precious mother, have been for me His most wonderful provision and the fountains of my greatest joy.

# II    PROVISION

# Acknowledgements

I wish to express my deep gratitude to Paul Jablonowski, Bill Eldridge, and Donna Fischer who reviewed the manuscript and made excellent editorial suggestions.

I am particularly grateful to Bill Eldridge for his great devotion to this project and the many hours he spent in prayer and anointed effort to help me bring this work to fruition. He has been a much appreciated "sounding board".

Special thanks also to Nirit Zagofsky for her dedicated editorial skills that have added immensely to the quality of the finished work.

My deep and enduring thanks also to Pastors Bob Johnson, Darrell Jones and Jerry Baughman and to Barbara Richmond who sponsored and engineered my first speaking tour to the United States and greatly encouraged me in this new ministry outreach.

Finally, many thanks to Harry and Brent Beecham for their faithful support of this project and my continuing ministry.

May the Lord God of Israel bless each of you as you have so abundantly blessed me.

# IV   PROVISION

# Table of Contents

## Part One
## First Encounters

# Part Two
# The Kaleidoscope

## Part Three
## Thorns Among the Cherries: Taking Up Our Everlasting Inheritance

# VIII   PROVISION

# Foreword

*Now also when I am old and grayheaded, O God,*
*do not forsake me, until I declare Your strength*
*to this generation, your power to everyone who is*
*to come.* (Ps 71:18)

For as long as I can remember, the Lord has visited me in a
recurring dream: a glorious vision of His almighty outstretched
hand holding me, as a small child, curled up in its hollow, secure,
utterly at peace in the protection of His love.

Now, in the autumn of my years, as I consider my life's journey thus far, I marvel at how, even in the midst of my innumer-
able failings and wanderings from His Way, He has been so
absolutely faithful to His promise:

> *"...Though the mountains be shaken and the hills*
> *be removed, yet my unfailing love for you will not*
> *be shaken nor my covenant of peace be*
> *removed," says the LORD, who has compassion*
> *on you.* (Isa 54:10) NIV

I am a Messianic Jew, one of a tiny minority of the ethnic
descendants of Jacob to whom, for reasons exclusively His own,
the Lord God of Israel, the God of Abraham, Isaac, and Jacob, has

seen fit by His grace to provide with the indescribable gift of redemption and eternal life by first drawing me close to Himself and then enabling me to embrace the wondrous, once and for all sacrifice of His only son, Yeshua.

For all of the days of my life, even before I ever knew Him personally, I have been aware, sometimes keenly so, of His protective presence, His guiding hand, His knowledge of my every thought, His mindfulness of even the smallest detail of the seeming minutiae of my life.

Certainly, from time to time He has allowed me to fall, but only, by the strength of His loving hand, to rise up again, each time having grown in my knowledge of Him, renewed and enabled with sufficient strength to continue the life's journey He carefully and lovingly ordained for me even before He had formed the earth.

> *When I consider Your heavens, the work of Your fingers, the moon and the stars, which You have ordained, what is man that You are mindful of him, and the son of man that You visit him?* (Ps 8:3-4)

How incredibly humbling and utterly amazing it is for me to now boldly declare in absolute truth — the Lord God of Israel, He Who created the heavens and the earth and all that is therein, has indeed, in His unfailing love and mercy, seen fit to *visit* me from time to time as I have traveled through the years of my life. Even from the first memories of my childhood, He has declared His Almighty presence with me through an utterly amazing galaxy of signs, wonders, and miracles that have illuminated my being and punctuated my every pathway. Always during the times of my greatest need, in those special euphoric moments when I have felt the tingling, intimate presence of His Holy Spirit;

during those everyday times when He has had something very special or even urgent to show me, even while I was totally immersed in the things of this world—never has He failed to pro-vision me with the very personal sign, wonder or miracle I have needed at that precise moment. From His heart to the depth of my awareness, He has always been there for me in this person-al, special way to encourage, protect, redirect, admonish or sim-ply to remind me of His unfathomable love and presence.

By no means do I consider myself in any way unique in hav-ing received these truly amazing heavenly visitations. His Word abounds with the promise of His unqualified availability to *all* those who would simply seek Him. He would exclude none from the pouring out of His signs, wonders and miracles, each gloriously, and very personally bearing witness to His almighty shepherding and infinitely loving presence.

Not a single ethnic Jew, the chosen of His first calling; nor a single Gentile, who by a simple act of faith might be grafted into the sacred and infinitely nourishing Jewish roots of the Body of Yeshua—absolutely none of these who diligently seek Him would He not so bless.

> *Seek the LORD and His strength; seek His face evermore! Remember His marvelous works which He has done, his wonders, and the judgments of His mouth, O seed of Abraham His servant, you children of Jacob, His chosen ones! He is the LORD our God; his judgments are in all the earth. And you will seek Me and find Me, when you search for Me with all your heart.* (Ps 105:4-7, Jer 29:13)

There is, however, another dimension, another stark reality in this supernatural relationship between our Creator and us, the people of His hand. We live in the world, where satan reigns as prince. Thus we remain, in a very real and intimate way, in constant peril from the fallout of an unrelenting battle being waged in heaven, a battle that began in the Garden of Eden where man first sinned.

> *For we do not wrestle against flesh and blood, but against principalities, against powers, against the rulers of the darkness of this age, against spiritual hosts of wickedness in the heavenly places.* (Eph 6:12)

It was there in the Garden, that God revealed His wonderful plan of redemption for all of His creation, a plan whose glorious conclusion will one day, soon I pray, be Yeshua's return to Israel.

Now, as we His Body wait for Him expectantly, we must be ever mindful that the enemy, satan and his legions of demons, have focused their every attention on two closely intertwined purposes. Never for a moment do they cease in their scheming to prevent the glorious second coming of our Lord Yeshua, all the while seeking at every turn to dismay, discourage and ultimately destroy His loving Body of believers, a Body that struggles to stay focused with excited anticipation upon Mount Zion.

Further, there is a clearly observable relationship between God's signs, wonders and miracles; and the level of satan's counter attention. The more God blesses in this truly remarkable way, the greater are satan's efforts to dismay, discourage and destroy. It is as if there were two synchronous supernatural rheostats: God's hand on one and satan's on the other.

> *Be sober, be vigilant; because your adversary the devil walks about like a roaring lion, seeking whom he may devour.* (1 Pet 5:8)

Certainly our God has the awesome power to snuff out satan in even less of an instant than it took Him to create the entire universe. In His perfect wisdom, however, He chooses not to do so—for now. I believe He thus allows the enemy to beset His people in order that He might teach them, mold them, and draw them ever closer to Himself. Such lifelong spiritual refining that the Word calls sanctification is a process that begins at the moment of our salvation in Yeshua and will continue until we finally meet Him face to face in glory.

I had a remarkable demonstration of this awesome, supernatural *modus operandi* just yesterday morning, when I took a break from my writing to stroll contemplatively about the streets of Tiberias. I often do this when I am seeking specific guidance. In this case I was pondering whether I should limit this recounting to just the good and pleasant things, thus showing my life in Him as a sort of divinely-filled "basket full of cherries," or, alternatively, if I should punctuate these wonderful, divine visitations with some of the stark and sobering satanic attacks over the years that have been aimed at my spiritual destruction. The Lord certainly made His desires in this regard abundantly and painfully clear. At the very moment I prayerfully sought His specific guidance on this point, I stepped off a curb, tripped, and literally fell flat on my face against the hard asphalt. Let me hasten to say that it wasn't the Lord who caused me to sustain a few painful abrasions and some lingering discomfort. Rather, it was He who simply *allowed* satan or one or more of his demons to give me a good solid shove just when it was needed. There is a central message in this.

> *And we know that all things work together for good to those who love God, to those who are the called according to His purpose.* (Rom 8:28)

Even as I grapple for some better understanding of this knowledge that is too wonderful for me to attain—even as I greatly yearn to take up my eternal residence in the mansion Yeshua has prepared for me in His Father's house, His Words cry out to the depth of my being:

> *Give to the LORD, O families of the peoples, give*
> *to the LORD glory and strength. Give to the LORD*
> *the glory due His name; bring an offering, and*
> *come into His courts.* (Ps 96:7-8)

Recently, I was very greatly blessed with a message brought by Reuven Ross, one of our pastors at Carmel Assembly in Haifa. One of Reuven's points especially spoke to my heart: As we strive to serve the Lord, we are called to give Him *all* the glory, *all* the glory due His mighty name. We must ever be aware of how satan so often steps in, encouraging us to keep just a little tiny bit of the glory for ourselves.

And so, dear reader, my heart quickens at the words of an angel:

> *Then I saw another angel flying in the midst of*
> *heaven, having the everlasting gospel to preach to*
> *those who dwell on the earth to every nation,*
> *tribe, tongue, and people saying with a loud*
> *voice, "Fear God and give glory to Him....."*
> (Rev 14:6-7)

The book you hold in your hands is an offering to Him who sits on the throne and unto the Lamb. May this recounting of but a few from the galaxy of signs, wonders and miracles with which He has so graciously provisioned me over the years while holding me in the hollow of His hand, at least  *begin* to give Him the glory due His name. May also these words, offered in His unfailing love,  encourage, build up, and otherwise bless the precious body of Yeshua and whomever else may read them.


RRF
Tiberias, Israel
January, 2001

# XVI  PROVISION

# Part One

# First Encounters

# Introduction

*He will feed His flock like a shepherd; he will gather the lambs with His arm, and carry them in His bosom.... And He took them up in His arms, put His hands on them, and blessed them.* (Isa 40:11a, Mark 10:16)

Ever since I first began contemplating the wonder of the heavens and who or what incredible, supernatural power might have set them out, I, surely like most of His creation, have been drawn to the seemingly eternal enigma of predestination versus free will. Has God ordered every single thought and moment of our lives? Are we entirely free to choose our own course? Or are we allowed some either defined or undefined constrained level of choice within the context of His pre-ordained parameters?

While pondering this enigma, I was once offered the following simple illustration:

> Consider a great ship proceeding between conti-
> nents. Its many passengers are free to scurry
> about its several decks, or to go anywhere else
> they may please within the physical confines of
> the vessel. While doing so, they are free to
> engage in any activity they may desire: to say  or
> do anything they may please; to believe what
> they may; to make whatever choices they desire.
> Nevertheless, inexorably, the ship will not be
> diverted from its passage from one shore to the
> other. All aboard  began their totally separate pas-
> sages from the same port, and likewise they all
> will arrive at a common destination.

For both theologians and secular philosophers, this enigma
has been the subject of endless debate and voluminous treat-
ments by the likes of Calvin, Schopenhauer and  countless others
since the very dawn of the written word. For me, the words written by the Holy Spirit through the Apostle Paul are sufficient.

> *For whom He foreknew, He also predestined to be*
> *conformed to the image of His Son, that He might*
> *be the firstborn among many brethren. Moreover*
> *whom He predestined, these He also called;*
> *whom He called, these He also justified; and*
> *whom He justified, these He also glorified.—-*
> *Blessed be the God and Father of our Lord Jesus*
> *Christ, who has blessed us with every spiritual*
> *blessing in the heavenly places in Christ, just as*
> *He chose us in Him before the foundation of the*
> *world, that we should be holy and without blame*

*before Him in love, having predestined us to adoption as sons by Jesus Christ to Himself, according to the good pleasure of His will, to the praise of the glory of His grace, by which He has made us accepted in the Beloved.* (Rom 8:29-30, Eph 1:3-6)

As a matter of my own conviction, I *know* that the Lord was intimately aware of my life in its every detail, even before He formed the earth. And like a passenger on the ship of our illustration, while I have been scurrying about the decks of my earthly existence all these years, He has not allowed me to deviate from the essential course of my journey. Even more, He has illuminated the sea lane of my life with a series of interspersed lighthouses to keep me safe along the way to protect me from running aground on the satanic shoals of evil placed there to entrap and destroy me. These, the lighthouses of His creation, are the signs, wonders, and miracles of which I now am called to speak.

I was the first of two sons born to totally devoted, deeply loving, greatly caring, entirely Jewish parents. Both feared God, but although it is not for me to judge, at least to my greatly sad understanding, neither were ever drawn to know Him personally.

My own ritual circumcision of the flesh, on the eighth day of my earthly existence, was the result of my religiously observant maternal grandmother Amelia's singular and emphatic insistence. My parents, Lillian and Alfred, told me years later that they had had no great concern about the matter one way or the other and had thus quickly assented in order to keep the peace.

Praise be to God for Grandma Amelia's insistence, the result of which was most certainly the first lighthouse miracle of my life! For with this act resulting from her singular conviction, my Jewishness was eternally sealed in obedience to the eternal covenant God made with Abraham and his descendants.

From that moment, I was forever spiritually as well as physically bonded with my people, chosen by God, and although for many ensuing years I was entirely unaware of the fact, I had in truth begun to take up my precious heritage.

# Chapter One

# Gertrude, Beauty and the Hollow of His Hand

*The God of my strength, in whom I will trust; my shield and the horn of my salvation, my strong-hold and my refuge; my Savior, You save me from violence. (2 Sam 22:3)*

I have often recalled, in the theater of my dreams, my  first remembered encounter with God's protection. Whether or not what I have repeatedly "seen" there is but a replay of the several times repeated  detailed account of the experience given to me by my parents over the years, or, as I am more inclined to believe, it has its genesis in an actual, clear, early childhood memory,  is really  of little significance. In either case, the vision of what happened is equally real and wonderful.

In the midst of the Great Depression that began in 1929, my father Alfred was greatly blessed to be offered employment as a technical manager with a then and still thriving, large and solid "blue chip"  company. There was, however,  according to Mr. Dan Green, an executive of the company and  my father's close friend of many years, only "one small problem."

Mr. Green *knew* my father was a Jew, and he was far more concerned about this reality of the flesh than was my father. Thus, as Mr. Green handed my father the application for employment, he suggested, "Al, you may not know this, but the company has an unwritten policy: we don't hire Jews. There are no exceptions. So if you don't want to be politely rejected, you would be well advised to act accordingly when you fill out this application."

Years later my father told me about his readiness to do what was required to get this badly needed job. "It really didn't matter at all to me," he related. "I simply wrote, 'Protestant' in the blank asking for religious preference.

"My father (your grandfather) did the same thing," he continued matter-of- factly. "His machine shop was located right in the heart of a very Christian neighborhood in Manhattan. All of his customers were Gentiles, and with a name like 'Fischer' that could 'go either way,' he found it easy to pass himself off as one of their kind."

And so it was that while so many others, Jews and Gentiles alike, marginally survived these terrible, depressed economic times by standing long hours in "bread lines," Alfred Fischer prospered to the extent that he was able to move my mother Lillian and me, a toddler just learning to walk into a posh apartment in then suburban Mount Vernon. He was even able to hire Gertrude, an experienced nanny, to help with my care and upbringing. Even more, in answer to my mother's pleading, Alfred acquiesced to purchase a family pet, a gorgeous, pedigreed female collie pup whom they aptly named Beauty. Even now, more than six decades later, I have deep and lingering warm memories of my immediate close bonding with these two wonderful new additions to our family.

The three of us, when the weather allowed, spent long hours together, wandering about the nearby, then very large and mostly undeveloped public park that bordered the Bronx River.

These were wonderful times, especially in the spring when everything was green and the wild flowers were blooming. I toddled along with Beauty always faithfully by my side as Gertrude, nearby, quietly supervised our wanderings as she basked in the nourishing warmth of the sun.

On one such delightful outing, however, the bucolic tranquillity being relished by the three of us came to a sudden and terrifying end. As I mindlessly toddled along in the unmowed grass, with Beauty in her usual place by my side, suddenly and without warning I stepped into a huge underground nest of yellow jackets. Within seconds I was covered with them from head to foot, and they were tormenting me, stinging me on every exposed part of my tender and terribly vulnerable 18-month-old body.

As I screamed in terror and pain, Beauty knew exactly what to do. She leaped upon me, knocking me to the ground, and then, protectively, she covered my entire body with her own, leaving my uppermost parts exposed just long enough for her to selflessly remove literally dozens of the torturing offenders from my face, head, and neck with her incessantly lapping tongue, all the while paying dearly for her heroic effort on my behalf as she was stung repeatedly wherever our attackers could find an exposed bit of flesh where her fur coat offered inadequate protection.

Gertrude immediately rushed to our rescue, herself being stung repeatedly as she pulled me out from under Beauty, took me in her arms and rushed the three of us to safety.

Had it not been for Beauty and Gertrude that day, I surely would have perished my life snuffed out even before it had a reasonable chance to begin. But God had a different plan for me than this. While it took several days for the three of us to recover from our terrifying and life threatening encounter, we were soon back to strolling again together in the park, although a bit more cautiously than on our earlier outings.

Alfred's career continued to prosper. He was promoted a few

months later and transferred (Grandma Amelia thought of it more as a "banishment") to the company's Portland, Oregon, office. We left Gertrude behind, and it was a sad parting for us all. Our beloved heroine, Beauty, went West with her family where she was to stand by my side for much of my ensuing childhood until finally she succumbed to her many years.

Where was the miracle in all this? Beyond the obvious fact that He put Gertrude and Beauty by my side to work out His divine protection, I am persuaded that He was already preparing me for the fallout I would later endure from the heavenly battle of the principalities that lay ahead in my life.

Even then He was molding me to understand that He would always be there for me, holding me protectively and at peace in the hollow of His hand, no matter the intensity of the turmoil in my midst.

What a divinely granted reassurance this was, given to me as a toddling child, as I now remain in a supernaturally provisioned peace, even while confronted with the savagery of a hellish *intifada* that would violently engulf the Israel of my inheritance; an insidious Holy War authored by the same satan who had placed the nest of yellow jackets in the pathway of my childhood so many years before.

# Chapter Two

# Of Furry Knees and Bobby's Christmas Scooter

*The LORD of hosts is with us; the God of Jacob*
*is our refuge. Selah* (Ps 46:11)

Alfred's promotion and accompanying transfer from New York to Portland, although loudly and woefully decried by Grandma Amelia as her son-in-law's personal plot against her happiness, provided fertile ground for us to be quickly accepted and easily absorbed into the almost exclusively Gentile Christian community in which we had been planted. There was a tragic albeit convenient irony in all this. We, a Jewish family who had purposefully donned Gentile masks in order to escape the negative social realities of our ethnic Jewishness, had been greatly facilitated in doing so by our unwitting immersion into a distinctly anti-Semitic new environment. There were few Jews in the Portland of the 1930s. I feel certain that scarcely any of our now fellow Oregonians had ever knowingly met or even seen one.

Nevertheless, as is the sad if not tragic tendency of humankind, most, certainly the majority, of our new neighbors had managed to develop and inculcate strong opinions about Jews: all of them highly negative. As the many blacks of those times were to the Southeastern United States, so then was the tiny minority of Jews to its Pacific Northwest.

For Alfred, apparently none of this had any immediate or deep importance. The ruse that had facilitated and had, so far, managed to sustain his employment, continued to work perfectly as his career and favor with a then notoriously anti-Semitic employer prospered all the more.

As for Lillian, while deeply missing the security and familiarity of her beloved New York, she nevertheless relished in her ready acceptance by her genuinely loving Christian neighbors who seemed to find her lifelong, deep, Bronx accent novel if not compelling.

For me, their precocious only son, certainly none of this mattered at the time. Like most Jewish children, I was genuinely adored, greatly loved, and showered with everything I could even remotely imagine or desire.

While my parents had never been, nor could then be open adherents to any expression of religious Judaism, they were nevertheless blessed with a seemingly inborn understanding and respect for the deepest ethical values of their heritage. Thus it was an easy reach for them to embrace the trappings of Christian celebration without necessarily giving any mind to any of its spiritual implications.

Christmas, for example, became a greatly anticipated annual family celebration of goodwill, genuine loving-kindness, and gift-giving.

From my earliest childhood memories of these happy family times, I was like any other excited child on Christmas morning. I had become totally integrated into the secular Christian world where I had been thus transplanted. And frighteningly, in at least some respects, I had insidiously already begun to inculcate many of its values and understandings.

It was on the fourth Christmas of my life, in the context of this entirely secular Christian world wherein I was being nurtured and reared, that the Lord God of Israel once again saw fit to manifest Himself to me in a most startling and unforgettable way.

On that particular Christmas morning, as I surveyed the many gifts designated for me beneath our large, traditional, brightly decorated tree, the one that stood out the most was a shiny, bright red, two-wheeled scooter. I could hardly wait for the gift unwrapping festivities to end so I could rush outside and give my now already most prized possession a proper initiation.

Our house, in an upper-middle-class neighborhood, was situated on a formidably elevated level, well above a not usually busy residential street. There was a driveway, perhaps fifty yards long, leading from the street upwards to a garage that was connected to the house. During the winter, when there was occasionally a skiff of snow or ice on the driveway, as was the case on this particular, marginally white Christmas, my father sometimes had a problem navigating the slope and instead, parked the family car along the street.

Since I had been "scooting" about the house, my parents apparently didn't notice when I slipped out the door with my new means of joyful conveyance in hand.

"Why not?" I asked myself as I surveyed the slope of the driveway before me. I trembled in anticipation as I began my rapid descent down the icy asphalt.

By the time I reached the street, I was screaming with both delight and fright; then suddenly, as I beheld and mentally processed the imminent and terrible threat to my very existence, I screamed in stark terror. I was going too fast to turn; I couldn't stop; I was absolutely out of control! Then I heard the squealing tires of the approaching panel delivery truck, as its equally terri-fied driver desperately tried to avoid contact with the scooter and its young rider that had  frighteningly and without warning, appeared before him.

Suddenly I found myself flying through space, as a phantas-magoric replay of my only four year existence flashed before my inner awareness. Violently I crashed, knees first to the pavement, then, leaving several layers of skin behind, I slid toward the oncoming vehicle! Finally, both I and it  stopped at the same moment. I smelled  burning rubber as  I  came to rest against a now unmoving tire. Then I briefly lost consciousness.

When I awoke a short time later, I found myself in the comfort of my father's strong arms. My mother was by his side, weeping in both fright and thanksgiving for my apparent survival. I saw the truck driver standing by her side visibly trembling and unable to speak.

The thing I remember most about my recovery from this near death experience are the enormous, thick, fuzzy scabs that entire-ly covered both of my  knees. It took several weeks for them to finally disappear, and still, today, I bear the physical scars of this experience.

I cannot begin to understand the full meaning God had in mind for me, my parents, and the driver of the panel truck on that most memorable of my Christmas mornings, but I can say it was soon thereafter that I started having an oft recurring dream about my being held in the protective hollow of God's almighty hand.

## Chapter Three

## Seeking after and Finding God
## The Miracle of Harvey Flansberg and a Band Uniform

*And Jesus said to him, "Today salvation has come to this house, because he also is a son of Abraham; for the Son of Man has come to seek and to save that which was lost."* (Luke 19:9-10)

I found myself totally lost as I walked aimlessly along the streets of an unfamiliar residential area in Vancouver, Washington, right across the Columbia River where we had recently moved from Portland. To this day, more than fifty years later, I still have a propensity to become disoriented, even in familiar surroundings.

It was late afternoon of an early autumn day, and I was filled with a sense of strangeness and unbelongingness on this first day of a new term, in a new school, in a new city. I had stayed after school to audition for the band, and I had thus missed the bus I had been told to take back to the house where I was staying for a few days with friends of our family while my parents were out of town. However disquieting, this "helplessly lost" aspect of my current situation seemed to me of only secondary importance. Sooner or later, I reasoned, I would find my way; surely someone would come along to direct me.

In my then fourteen-year-old thinking, I had a far more urgent need than simply to find my way. It seemed I had just, this very afternoon, to my amazement and delight been selected to play first chair clarinet in the Shumway Jr. High School Band. Mr. Harvey Flansberg, the band's director, who had been gracious enough to select me, had informed us band members that mandatory practices were to begin that very evening and continue with intensity each evening thereafter until the close at hand first football game of the season when we would make our musical debut. Mr. Flansberg had further instructed that it would be absolutely necessary for all the new members, like myself, to immediately purchase band uniforms from a shop he designated in the city and further, that we were to appear in them no later than at tomorrow evening's practice.

I was at once totally thrilled and dismayed: thrilled by my selection, and dismayed by my seeming inability to comply with Mr. Flansberg's explicit instructions.

The smart looking uniform, consisting of a brass buttoned blue jacket and white trousers would cost twenty dollars, no small amount of money in 1948. The problem was that my parents had left me only a small amount of lunch money, not nearly enough to purchase the required uniform. Thus, as I ambled aimlessly along, I desperately tried to conjure up some solution to my seemingly unsolvable problem.

Suddenly it occurred to me that it might help if I prayed—an activity I had never seriously engaged in up to this point in my young life. I immediately dismissed this notion as futile, as my mind raced back over the events of the past several years events that had been traumatic enough in my reckoning to convince me that there was no supernatural power to whom I could turn for help. For me, the concept of God was fanciful. He did not exist, at least not for me.

Then, despite my conscious resistance, my thoughts, as they often did, once again returned to the still painful and as yet unresolved trauma I had endured some seven years earlier. There, in an insistent and unrelenting replay of a memory I struggled unsuccessfully to suppress, I found myself once again sitting with my mother in a Pullman compartment of a train just pulling out of the Portland station, a train that would carry us back to New York on our first visit there in the five years since we had moved West.

I was seven years old, and, while many other relatives on both sides of the family had expressed their desire for us to return to New York, Grandma Amelia had been absolutely unrelenting in making known her growing displeasure and outright demand to see her daughter and grandson. Alfred's tongue-in-cheek declaration that he "could not take time from his work" to accompany us was of little concern to either him or Grandma Amelia. For my father, the best place in the world for him to be was that which was most distant from his mother-in-law. And from Grandma Amelia's perspective, it was Alfred who was personally to blame for "ruining her life" by removing her darling daughter and only grandson from her immediate presence. It was thus, on the condition he would *not* be required to participate, that my father had finally succumbed to Grandma Amelia's insistence and allowed the two of us to make this extended visit back to the Bronx, a visit that would begin just before *Pesach* (the Jewish Passover) in April, and end just after my eighth birthday in mid-June.

There was, however, from Alfred's perspective, another

benefit in his staying on the job in Portland. My mother had thereby assumed  sole responsibility for dealing with a very sensitive situation involving me, their son. It was a most uncomfortable thing she had been called to do, and she wasted no time getting to it.

"Bobby, you are  a big boy," she began tentatively as the train pulled out of the station and began to gain momentum. She took my hands in her own. "You are now old enough to know—" she hesitated, struggling to find the right words, "a sort of family secret," she continued after having paused just long enough to add a sense of mystery to what she was about to reveal.

"What are you talking about, Mom?" I replied cautiously, growing frightened as I studied her very expressive face,  trying to catch some preview of what she might be trying to tell me. What I saw in her almost transparent countenance was at once a deeply troubling and totally uncharacteristic blend of compassion, regret, and fear.

Sensing my rising alarm, she got right to the point. "Bobby," she continued matter-of-factly, "the family secret is—you are," she almost whispered the word, "Jewish."

I was flabbergasted far too deeply shocked to audibly respond. *Me, a Jew?* I tried to assimilate the reality of this what was to me an unthinkable possibility, but I couldn't take it in.

"*Me, a Jew?*" I finally blurted out in profound disbelief, horror, then denial, trying at once to both process and reject my mother's revelation in the face of my own already well developed  environmentally induced anti-Semitic  underpinnings.

"You can't tell anyone about this," she continued, alarmed by my dramatic reaction to her revelation, "your father's job depends on this!"

I was in shock, utterly unable to respond further as the remainder of my mother's well-intentioned and well-rehearsed words  attempted to explain how all this had come about and to prepare me for what was soon to come.

"We will be arriving just in time for *Pesach*," she explained, trying to make this sound like something positive, "and we will be spending this wonderful holiday with Grandma Amelia and all of my closest family. Sensing that I didn't understand, she started to explain the highly significant meaning of this Jewish remembrance. "*Pesach*," she began but, by now, the input channels of my brain had grown numb from what I had already heard and I could take in no more.

Suddenly, something I did not immediately perceive through any of my physical senses snapped me back to the seemingly deserted residential Vancouver street and into a once-again stark awareness of my current desperate situation. I had become mysteriously *aware* of "something" undefined that had piqued my interest.

Fearfully I conjectured, trying to suppress my rising panic as I once again took in the reality of my present situation: how much further had I wandered into the unknown depths of this unfamiliar city while I had been so deeply lost in my unpleasant recollections? Then, despite my effort to resist, I found myself slipping back into their grasp.

I, Bobby Fischer, the greatly adored "prodigal" grandson, sat in a place of honor at Grandma Amelia's symbol-laden traditional *Pesach* table. It was *all* there: the bitter herbs, the hard-boiled egg, the lamb bones, the sweet *charoset*, but I understood none of it. Instead, I was a most unwilling participant, nearly overwhelmed by my intense desire to escape, not only from my present surroundings, but also from the unacceptable reality of whom and what I had so suddenly and shockingly become. *Me, a Jew??*

"Nu, everything is ready," Grandma Amelia pronounced in her

heavily Yiddish- accented English, as she solemnly  began the *Pesach seder* by lighting the *Shabbat* candles.

Then, almost at once, she corrected her earlier pronouncement. "Everything is ready but one thing," she continued, turning to her live-in, unmarried brother Nathan whom everyone called Uncle Jim. "Jimmie," she commanded,  "you should please *help* Bobby."

At this, I watched as Uncle Jim retrieved something that he had been holding in his lap from under the table.

He moved quickly toward me, and, before I could visibly react, he had placed a white *kippa* upon my head and a traditional prayer shawl about my shoulders.

"Now, Bobby," Grandma Amelia proudly proclaimed, "you look like a *real* Jewish boy!"


Once again I found myself  snapped back into the present reality: lost in a strange city, beset by a seemingly unsolvable problem.

"Oh God!" I cried out at the painful horror of my recollection, but there was no one there in the loneliness of this seemingly deserted Vancouver street to hear me.

"Oh God!" I cried out again more loudly than before, at first pleadingly, then angrily when I suddenly remembered my set-in-concrete conclusion that there really was no God.

"Who do you think you are crying out to?" I asked  myself bitterly. Then, mockingly, out of my deep hurt and frustration,  as if to prove a point, I prayed out loud, mouthing the words of a petition for the first time in my life.

"Oh, God," I cried out again in the framework of a proposed covenant that flooded into my mind " If you *really* exist and can *actually* hear me, then *answer* me! I need a miracle! Get me a band uniform  and I will *believe* in you forever!" Suddenly, in the very next instant following my outburst, the earlier perceived "something" I had been unable to define with my senses took on recognizable earthly dimensions. What I now physically saw was *someone* very far ahead of me, walking in the same direction down this same totally unfamiliar street. Inexplicably, this person who only a moment before had been indistinguishable, now looked strangely familiar. Something within told me to hurry ahead to catch up with whomever it might be. I began to walk fast, then faster, and then I started running. As I drew closer, I next perceived that this person was a man. Then, moments later, I was overcome by the amazing reality of my perception. "Oh my God!" I now cried out in utter disbelief. This man ahead of me was unmistakably Mr. Harvey Flansberg. He was dressed in his band director's uniform, the very same kind of uniform I so desperately required and just moments before had pleaded with God to provide.

As I quickly closed the small, remaining distance between us, something deep within me confirmed that I was in the midst of receiving an unmistakable miracle. I had pleaded with God for a very special favor, and, to my absolute and utter amazement, He had undeniably and immediately answered.

Mr. Flansberg was carrying a large and bulky bundle. As he soon explained, this special bundle happened to be a number of surplus used band uniforms left over from previous years that he had just discovered in a storeroom at school and had decided to bring home for some possible future use.

Within moments we were standing in Mr. Flansberg's living room. It seems I had caught up with him right in front of his home just as he was about to turn into its entrance. I quickly explained my situation to him, and there I was, not fully able to take in the sheer wonder of this moment; there I was, actually trying on one of these precious surplus uniforms. It fit me perfectly. Mr. Flansberg said with a smile, "consider it yours. "Let me drive you to where you are staying," he said, "so you will have time to get something to eat and change into your uniform before  band practice."

In that incredible, first offered then immediately answered prayer, I had joyfully accepted the reality of God, and I had begun to seek His Almighty presence in my life.

## Chapter Four

## Another Walk Through the Valley of the Shadow

*Have mercy on me, O LORD, for I am weak; O
LORD, heal me, for my bones are troubled. My
soul also is greatly troubled; but You, O LORD—
how long?* (Ps 6:2-3)

The stabbing pain exploded in pulsing crescendos just behind
my shoulder blades; then it radiated  torturing electric-like shock
waves that  coursed along seemingly every nerve in my body.  It
was early November, 1979. I was  deputy commander of the
largest group in the United States Air Forces Europe, a high point
in my already long, exciting, and greatly gratifying military career.
But none of this mattered at the moment, only the overwhelming
pain  from which there seemed to be no escape.

Only a few hours earlier, I  had been admitted to the neurosurgical ward of Landsthul Army Hospital, Germany, and I had
just undergone an extensive series of, in themselves torturous,
diagnostic procedures. The medication I had finally been given

had just begun to take hold, but my heart was still pounding in my chest from my long day of pain filled trauma.

I had been aware for some time that there was something terribly wrong, but I had been too totally occupied with my work, and, more truthfully, too terrified to do anything "official" about the recurring episodes of stabbing pain that had been becoming more frequent and intense.

Then, just this morning, as I had been about to present an important highly classified briefing to a group of high ranking NATO Alliance officers, I had suddenly collapsed in excruciating pain. Now I had no choice. Unable to drive myself, a co-worker had rushed me to the nearby Sembach Air Base Clinic. There, three flight surgeons wasted no time. They examined me, in turn, and then huddled in the corner to privately discuss their findings. They seemed to remain in this conference forever, and I grew impatient as the pain, after just a brief respite, once again returned.

"Hey, you guys!" I protested. "What's going on??"

The three immediately approached me where I lay stretched out on a nearby gurney. One of them acted as a spokesman.

"Colonel Fischer," he began in his well-practiced, most professional voice, "you have what could be a serious problem in your cervical spine; you need to be admitted to the hospital immediately."

"How serious?" I responded, trying to put on the bravest possible face. "Please be honest with me; what do you think is wrong?"

The spokesman took me at my word and answered forthrightly: "Something is compressing your spinal cord. You need to have a complete neurological work-up to determine what it is and how to proceed."

"You didn't answer my question," I protested. "*What* do you think it is that is compressing my spinal cord?"

"We believe it is likely you may have a tumor on your cord," he responded matter-of-factly.

"If it's a tumor, what are the chances that it is malignant?" I further inquired, still trying to maintain some outward appearance of strength in order to conceal the stark terror that had begun to consume me along with the now-returned, terrible pain.

"These kinds of tumors are most often malignant," he replied. Then, anticipating my next question, he continued, "They are usually inoperable."

"I need to call my wife," I mumbled, my mask of bravery torn away by the just conveyed, devastating news. I managed with considerable difficulty to pull myself off the gurney and hobble to a nearby phone.

It was this telephone call to Donna, my beloved wife of then 19 years, that clearly marked the beginning of what was to be my most miraculous healing.

Donna is a highly skilled and greatly experienced critical care registered nurse. It was by no small coincidence that she happened to be employed by Landsthul Army Hospital at that time, and that she had made it her business to be very well acquainted with the entire surgical staff as well as their various levels of individual competency.

She, too, struggled to put on her best professional demeanor as I explained my frightening situation. However, her love for me and her wifely concern overcame her attempt as it became obvious to me from her lovingly familiar voice that she was choking back tears.

"Sweetheart," she insisted knowingly, "there are several neurosurgeons on the staff, but the *only* one you should see is Doctor Tom Carter. I'll call him right now if you like."

I sensed that someone or something was trying to pull me

back into an awareness of my surroundings. I struggled to rise up through the drug induced fog that had dulled my sensibilities even while it numbed my now just-returning waves of electric shock-like incessant pain.

"Colonel Fischer," I felt someone gently shaking my shoulder. I opened my eyes tentatively, trying to take in my immediate surroundings. "It's me, Doctor Carter. How are you feeling?"

I looked up and struggled to focus on the strikingly handsome Afro-American face of Thomas Edward Carter, M.D., the neurosurgeon of Donna's choice, who had been my admitting physician several hours earlier.

"Much better," I was able to respond after a moment of shaking my head to clear my thinking, "the medications have helped a lot."

"Bob," he began. He used my first name in a personal, intimate sort of way that transmitted his genuine concern and deep interest in my well-being. I had been immediately drawn to him that morning when we first met and he examined me, then sent me on a round of diagnostic studies. Donna had been so right. Tom Carter was someone very special. I could sense his deep concern and compassion. I was in the presence of a healer and I immediately entrusted myself to him.

"I've looked at all your test results and we've got to talk about the options," he continued.

I had been fearing the worst, and I dared to boldly venture "Do I have a tumor?"

He smiled reassuringly, "*No*, you don't," he replied emphatically, "this isn't cancer, but you do have another serious problem, something we need to deal with very soon."

What could be more serious than a malignant tumor, I conjectured, as I found myself suddenly overcome with relief. My reprieve, however, was to endure for only a brief moment.

Doctor Carter went on, trying to explain my condition in lay terms that I could understand. "Bob, you've got a disease we call cervical spondylosis, what amounts to arthritis of the spinal vertebra. There are arthritic spurs—bone growth, along the entire length of your spinal column."

I tried to understand the seriousness of what he was saying, but still found myself unable to stop rejoicing in the reality that I had a new lease on life—I didn't have *cancer*!

"In your particular case," he went on, "there has been a traumatic and life- threatening development."

I could only muster a sighed "*ohhh??*" as my momentary lease on life had once again been rudely foreclosed.

"The cervical disc at the C-6, C-7 level has slipped out of place, then calcified. It is now pressing up against another arthritic bony growth called a 'bone bar' that runs right along the cord. As a result, the cord in turn is not only seriously compressed but there are tiny fragments from the bone bar that have actually invaded the cord itself." He paused, looking for some response, and, when he found nothing but my continuing stunned silence, he went on.

"This cord compression and invasion are what is causing not only your severe pain, but also, just in case you haven't noticed," he smiled soothingly, reassuringly, somehow easing my rising panic, " you have lost a great deal of your strength in all four of your extremities, and there has also been a considerable amount of sensory loss."

I had begun to take in the profound seriousness of my situation and was finally able to respond, questioningly. "What are the options, I asked?" fearing the worst.

"If you had asked me this a month ago," Doctor Carter replied, trying not to sound overly optimistic, "I would have told you that your condition was inoperable and that the only course was to suppress your pain while you grew steadily worse. In all likelihood, you would have certainly soon been confined to a wheel chair, and then, well—"

I interrupted, "You seem to be telling me that there is some other approach???"

"Yes, Bob, I am," he replied,  at first hesitantly, then, despite himself, exuding his own excitement. "I've just returned from a three-week sabbatical in Switzerland where I had the privilege of working with one of the world's leading neurosurgeons. He has been developing a whole new approach to our profession, something called microsurgery,  a very delicate surgical technique performed under a powerful Zeiss Microscope. The technique is still entirely experimental, although it has been employed in a few very closely controlled cases, all of them much less complex than your own."

"Why are you telling me this, doctor?" I probed, trying to find some confirmation of hope for myself, however slight, in all this.

"Bob, I think there is some chance I can help you with this." He paused, trying to find just the right words before he went on. "I want you to understand that I have never  employed this technique before, nor has my Swiss colleague ever used it in  a situation anywhere near as complex as your own."

"Be more specific," I pleaded , "just what do you see as a probable outcome?"

This was the opportunity he had been setting up. "Bob, there is a good chance that you might not survive the surgery. If you do, then it is likely you will be a quadriplegic, or, more optimistically  a paraplegic."

I interrupted before he could continue. "Where is the hope in this?" I begged.

He smiled cautiously, trying not to convey any false expectations. "There is always a chance that you could walk away from this—it would take a miracle, but miracles do happen. I'll tell you what," he went on, gently shutting off  for the moment any further discussion. "Let's meet in my office tomorrow morning at ten. I've asked Donna to be there; I want to show you both exactly what I have in mind." With that, he smiled, and exuding great warmth and confidence, he stood and left the room.


"This is your cervical spine," Doctor Carter began, pointing to an illuminated x-ray as Donna and I listened attentively at the appointed hour the next morning in the small Neurosurgical Ward office. "You can see these clear protrusions from every vertebra." Then, pointing to the clearly visible calcified disc and bone bar, he explained, "Here is the immediate problem."

"Let me show you what I propose," he continued professionally. "I would approach the afflicted area from the front by making an incision here," he said touching his own throat. "This is a very crowded part of the anatomy," he went on. "By the way, are you a singer??"

I was puzzled by his question. "Well, I do love to get into the hymns at chapel, but beyond that, no. Why do you ask?"

"There are two nerves that control the larynx," he explained somewhat soberly, "one entering from each side. In order to access the operative site, I will have to sacrifice one of these nerves. As a result, your voice will be quite gruff and relatively low in volume. You will find singing, or excessive talking painful, if not impossible.

He tried to de-emphasize the seriousness of this revelation, seeing my obvious concern. "But this is the least of your problems right now," he continued. "Besides, we are beginning to do all sorts of things with nerve grafting, and we may be able to go back in and repair this later."

"Okay," I responded matter-of-factly, trying to appear strong in the face of this latest startling revelation.

"Once I get to the site," he went on, "I will remove the calcified disc and the bone bar. Then comes the critical and intensely delicate phase." He paused a moment, then went on.

"Next, using the Zeiss microscope, I will very carefully attempt to  remove all the invading fragments from the cord without causing any more damage than you have already sustained. Finally, I will reconstruct your cervical spine using a bone plug for support that I will remove from your right hip. That's about it, he concluded."

"How long will the procedure take?" Donna asked,  trying not very successfully to sound professional.

"I estimate a minimum of  ten hours," Doctor Carter responded, rising to her attempt, now speaking in a different tone, one professional to another. "This is a very complex, almost entirely new procedure."

"When would you like to do this?" I asked, having already made a tentative decision.

"I've scheduled the operating room for early tomorrow morning," he said, looking for my consent to proceed.

Donna and I exchanged deep and searching glances. I could sense at once  her great concern,  deep resolve, and profound love. As we embraced,  I could feel her trembling in my arms.

"Let's do it!" I said.

Donna left for home at eight that evening with the promise that she would return later to work the night shift,  which would end just in time for her to be with me before my surgery early the next morning.

Robin, our first-born was in Munich where she was a freshman at the University of Maryland extension. We had decided not to alarm her by telling her anything about my urgent situation.  We could not avoid sharing my situation with our other two daughters, Cindy, then seventeen, and Julie, fifteen, who were living at home. I had tried to comfort them the best I could when they visited me that afternoon, but they  were already beside themselves with worry and concern.

After Donna left, I lay there, quietly thanking God for having so greatly blessed me with these four precious women who had so completely brightened my life. We were a very close and loving family, and I was quietly delighting in how precious they each were to me.

"Good evening, Colonel Fischer," an unexpected visitor interrupted. Without waiting for a response, he made his way to the chair beside my bed and sat down.

"I'm Father Ed Riordan, one of the hospital chaplains," he introduced himself. "I understand you have a big day scheduled tomorrow, and I've come by to pray with you if you'd like."

"I'm not a Catholic," I responded with sincere gratitude, "but I would certainly welcome your prayers."

He offered a tentative explanation. "It looks like someone messed up your 'religious preference' on the admission paperwork. Really, if you'd rather not...."

"*Please*, Chaplain," I assured my visitor, "I really mean it; "It doesn't hurt to cover all the bases."

I sensed his genuine warmth, concern, and compassion as he made the sign of the cross and began, "In the name of the Father and the Son and the Holy Ghost ...."


As this priest prayed, I was once again caught up in my vivid recollections.

I was eighteen, and a freshman at the University of Rochester, passionately intent upon finally achieving the object of my long quest. For all of these several years I had sought to learn more about God. I *knew* He existed and was mindful of me. Ever since years earlier, when He had miraculously provisioned me with a band uniform, I had yearned deeply to *know* Him more personally, to establish a genuine relationship with Him. Yet, I admonished myself, I must have been looking in all the wrong places because I had somehow failed to find Him. More than a few obviously well-intentioned  people, including some of my closest friends and even  total strangers, had tried to convince me that such a personal relationship with God could only be achieved through Jesus Christ, who they claimed was Himself  God. I had, each time,  immediately rejected the very idea that a man could also be God. Still,  I deeply hungered for more understanding. Finally,  I was  persuaded  to  investigate  the  Roman  Catholic Church where I was assured He might be found.

Father John Merklinger, became my mentor and teacher in the ways of the Church. We had been meeting in long sessions two evenings each week for the previous six weeks,  and  this was  to be the last of our scheduled times together.

Father John, as he liked to be called, although I sensed  he was doing his best to conceal his feelings, had understandably  grown deeply  frustrated  with  the  questioning  and  even  combative young person who sat before him in his comfortable study.

The usual outcome of such an intensive six week orientation into the ways and beliefs of the Church was conversion. While he had met with considerable success with previous candidates, it was obvious to Father John that his present charge was anything but close to such a commitment. It wasn't an easy thing to allow this lost soul to remain among the unsaved.

"Bob," he asked imploringly, "since this is to be our last meeting, at least for now, would you please tell me, if you can, what it is about the Church and its teachings you  find  difficult to embrace? Maybe if we  face these obstacles together, I could help you  get beyond them."

I had grown very fond of this deeply devoted man during our many hours together, yet  he had opened a door, and my continuing frustration poured forth in response.

"Father John," I began, "there are several teachings of the Church I simply am unable to embrace...."

"That's it, Bob," he interrupted encouragingly, "lay them all out so we can deal with them——."

And so I did, recognizing that he would accept nothing less than my full candor.

"If Jesus Christ is the Son of God and God Himself," I pleaded, "then I have been unable to find Him here. How can I accept Him as God if I've never met Him?"

He hesitated for a moment, collecting his thoughts, then responded fervently. "You *can* find Him, Bob, right here in the Church! He appointed the Apostle Peter to be His vicar here on earth—to reign over us all, to sit on His throne in His place! Every successive Pope," he went on, "even now, the Holy Father in Rome—He is our 'Christ' on earth!"

"Bless you now, my son," said the hospital chaplain concluding his lengthy prayer as he once again made the sign of the cross and stood, preparing to continue his rounds. "May He carefully watch over you and Doctor Carter tomorrow."

I offered a simple "Thank you" as he quietly left my room, and I instantly fell back asleep.

"Hey, Bob!" I was again awakened a short time later. "What are you trying to pull," Chaplain Dick Knowles offered by way of greeting as he touched my shoulder warmly and took the seat recently vacated by the hospital chaplain.

Richard K. Knowles was one of three Protestant chaplains assigned to Sembach Air Base Chapel where Donna, the girls, and I regularly attended. He was my favorite of the three, and I was immediately grateful for the very real comfort I already felt from his visit.

"Looks like I've really done it this time, Dick," I responded, trying to make light of my truly grave situation. "I thought I'd take a few days off...."

He immediately saw through my feigned jocularity. "I know things are pretty tough, Bob, but I know also that you love the Lord and that He loves you. Let's ask Him for His healing presence tomorrow."

"Amen," I replied as I bowed my head and this dear man of God began to intercede on my behalf.

Yes, I did indeed love Jesus Christ, my Lord and my God. I had finally and joyfully met Him face to face in another Air Force Protestant Chapel, some twenty-one years earlier. Now, as Dick Knowles prayed, I found myself once again in that very chapel, at McChord Air Force Base near Tacoma, Washington, on the glorious day when I had sealed my faith with baptism. Chaplain Erwin Ray, a Methodist, who had spent many hours patiently leading me to the Lord, was just concluding this precious celebration of my entry into the Kingdom of God as he intoned:

> "Having been buried with Christ in baptism, you are raised to live a new life... 'applying all diligence, in your faith supply moral excellence, and in your moral excellence, knowledge; and in your knowledge, self-control, and in your  self control, perseverance, and in your perseverance, godliness; and in your godliness, brotherly kindness, and in your brotherly kindness, love...for as long as you practice these things, you will never stumble; for in this way the entrance into the eternal kingdom of our Lord and Savior Jesus Christ will be abundantly supplied to you.'"

Now many years later, as I recalled from the confines of my hospital bed,  this beginning of my walk with Jesus  Christ,  I reflected on how very true He had been  to His sacred  promise. He had indeed abundantly supplied my every need, both spiritual and material. Joyfully,  I knew  there could be no question as to which had been  greatest of all these many blessings.

I had  fallen head over heals in love with Second Lieutenant Donna Jean Goade from the  moment I had first caught sight of her sitting across from me one Friday afternoon "Happy Hour"  at the Eglin Air Force Base Florida Officers' Club. A whirlwind courtship had followed our first meeting. I was, at the time, permanently stationed at a small radar site in Northern California and on temporary assignment  at Eglin for just six weeks. Thus, after we met, Donna and I had  spent every available free moment together.

This short time  rushed by, and now, on the evening before I was to depart, I knew that I was hopelessly in love. The few short hours before our impending separation tugged at my heart, an unacceptable reality.

A full moon lit up the night, and it seemed like every star in the heavens was on glorious display just for us as we walked arm in arm along the silver sand of the exquisitely beautiful northern Florida beach. We sat down on a large piece of driftwood and cuddled close together as we watched the intermittently crashing surf. The water was phosphorescent, made literally alive from myriad  iridescent algae.

I  knew beyond all doubt;  this precious woman whom I now held close had been appointed to be my lifelong wife by the very God we both greatly loved. Even so, something deep within held me back from being overly confident that she would have me as her husband.

Yes, I reasoned, as I struggled  to find just the right words, I *had* cast aside what had been an incredible burden for most of my life! Never mind the reality of my ethnic heritage, I had never really acknowledged my Jewishness, and now I had formally discarded it in favor of another faith, another belief system that had already become the lighthouse of my life. I had, in my thinking, superseded my Jewishness when I unreservedly embraced Jesus Christ as my Messiah. Surely, I prayed, she will understand this, as I left her side and knelt in the silver sand before her.

"Donna," I began, "there is no other way to say this;" I love you with all my heart, and I simply can't go through the rest of my life without you." I could see the joy of acceptance in her eyes even before I asked, "Will you marry me??"

She didn't hesitate, even for a moment. "Of course I will, Darling," she replied as tears of joy illuminated by the glowing night began to course down her cheeks.

"There is one thing I haven't told you—" I almost whispered apologetically, "something you really need to know—"

She kissed me, her total trust filling me with a confidence to which I desperately tried to cling in the fond hope that what I was about to reveal would not make any *real* difference.

"You know that I love the Lord with all my heart, but what you don't know—" I hesitated.

"What *are* you talking about," she interrupted, not taking me seriously.

I rushed to the point, fearfully believing that all I now held dear was in imminent and terrible jeopardy.

"Donna," I said, trying to keep down my rising emotion "Like you, I'm a Christian, but unlike you, I was *born* a Jew. Both of my parents are Jewish."

She didn't hesitate for even a brief moment to consider what I had so dreadfully offered. Instead she responded simply and with absolute sincerity, "Jewish!—Bob, that's *wonderful!*

"How is Donna handling all this," Dick Knowles asked sympathetically, pulling me back to the reality of the moment.

"Just like the perfect Air Force wife she is," I replied, not even trying to conceal my genuine pride. "I married a real trooper!"

"We'll all be praying for you, Bob, and for Donna and the girls as well," Dick offered, as he stood, stooped down and gave me a brotherly hug. Then, as he headed out the door he blessed me greatly by asserting what I already knew in the depths of my heart.

"God bless you and keep you my brother. Never forget that He is with you."


Bill Stroebel was a Systems Development Corporation technical representative to my Tactical Control Group. Thus I frequently worked with him professionally. Bill's wife Beverly and Donna were good friends, and the four of us were very active together in the Protestant Chapel program. Our daughter Robin, and their eldest, Carrie, were then and to this day remain best friends. At the time, they were college roommates in Munich.

It was therefore not surprising to me that Bill and Bev were with Donna the next morning when she came to sit with me until it was time for an orderly to wheel me away to the operating room. What I didn't know until days later was that these two dear friends would then sit with Donna, praying almost constantly during most of what turned out to be the long twelve hours I remained under Tom Carter's most delicate and intensive care.

"Bob, count backwards beginning at one hundred," Tom Carter instructed, as he stared at me intently, searchingly. I began to count, "100, 99, 98 " The green surgical head covering provided a somehow beautiful and elegant frame for the classically handsome, mahogany colored face of this natural and greatly gifted healer whom I knew had been provided by God. I felt a surge of confidence and intense warmth that was somehow transmitted by his large and deeply probing eyes as I began to slip away into oblivion.

There she was! How typical for her to have chosen this place, I reflected joyfully seeing my mother Lillian sitting there in a seemingly unending meadow covered with a blanket of the most incredibly beautiful flowers I had ever seen. They are poppies, I deduced, brilliant, golden poppies with an intensity of color that was beyond any human ability to perceive, much less describe. Yet, I *was* somehow perceiving them and I was filled with an overwhelming intensity of joy and peace that could only have flowed from the very throne of God.

I had been crushed, even devastated by my mother's sudden death from a massive heart attack. It had already been thirteen years since she collapsed in her own bed of beautiful, golden-colored chrysanthemums. Alfred, my brother Marty, and I placed on her grave the bouquet she had been picking when she had collapsed.

"Mom!" I cried out as I ran towards her. She looked remarkably beautiful and totally at peace.

"Bobby! My Bobby!" she exclaimed joyfully, standing and opening her arms.

"I knew you would be coming," she said as we met and embraced. We walked along together among the indescribably beautiful golden poppies, talking, sharing.

Then, just as suddenly as I had happened on this amazing scene, it began to fade from my perception. I struggled to stay there. "No, no, I "

"Bob, Bob!" Someone was rudely calling my name. I tentatively opened my eyes and once again beheld Doctor Tom Carter's remarkably handsome face and intense eyes.

I was suddenly aware that he was holding my left hand in his own. "Bob," wiggle your fingers," he gently commanded. I complied and saw  the intensity of his probing gaze begin to soften. He took  my  other  hand  in  his  own,  repeating  his  instruction. "Wiggle your fingers, Bob!" I did! His eyes now began to transmit the beginnings of  joy, yet still only tentatively.

He moved to the  end of the gurney and lifted one of my feet with his hands. "Wiggle your toes, Bob!"  His voice conveyed a bizarre blend of hopeful anticipation offset by a dreadful willingness to accept failure. As my toes began to move strongly in his hands, his  remarkable eyes began to dance with joy. He quickly transferred his grasp  to my other foot, repeating his instruction to which I  immediately complied. Tom Carter's entire face, the remarkably  handsome  face  of  God's  chosen  healer,  was  now overcome with a blend of unabashed thanksgiving and the sheer joy of professional accomplishment.

"You are going to be just fine, Bob," he proclaimed, trying to remain at least somewhat professional by holding back his obviously deep emotion. "You've gotten your miracle!"

Even though my post-surgical recovery had been amazingly fast and nearly complete, Doctor Carter had never the less presented me with the option of a full medical retirement, a retirement that would provide me with a generous tax-free pension. He based this offer on both the neurological deficits that remained, which he felt would be permanent, and on his prognosis that I could certainly expect a continuing series of such surgeries,  the next of which could even be imminent.

Although I now walked with a profound limp due to  a pronounced motor weakness in my right leg and  had a corresponding sensory impairment in my left leg, I begged my doctor in my earlier promised, now barely discernible gruff voice. "Please, Doctor Carter, I want to stay on active duty. I love the Air Force and I can't bear the thought of leaving if there is any way I can stay on."

"Okay," he agreed reluctantly, "but only on the condition that you stay in close touch wherever we both may be over the next few years. You are a remarkable patient to say the least, and I want to follow your progress."

"And believe me, Doctor Carter, if I have to travel to the end of the earth, if and when I need another operation, no one but you is going to get the job."

My remarkable survival and initial recovery from this surgical "valley of the shadow of death" was only the beginning of what was to be a continuing miracle.

As I completed the remaining seven months of my European tour of duty, the Air Force gave me the assignment of our dreams. We were sent back to Phoenix, Arizona, from where we had departed nearly five years earlier, and were able to move back into our lovely house there that we had rented during our long absence.

I had a wonderful new job as Director of Operations and Plans for the 26th North American Air Defense Command Region, and we were once again able to continue our very active participation in the Luke Air Force Base Chapel program.

What a blessed time this was for me, Donna, and the girls. I was the one whom the chaplains called on to give the sermon on Lay Sunday, and I was greatly blessed to serve as head usher, Sunday school teacher and in whatever other capacity they might require.

Donna relished her new job in the critical care unit of Boswell Hospital in the retirement community of nearby Sun City. She often stopped on her way to or from work to visit Alfred who had purchased an apartment there soon after we returned to

Arizona.

Robin continued her college education at nearby Arizona State University, and Cindy began hers at Northern Arizona University at Flagstaff. Julie was to follow Robin at Arizona State two years later.

Doctor Tom Carter, who had been an Air Force major when we first met so fatefully, had transferred to the Army and was now a full Colonel and head of Neuro-Surgery at Fitzsimons Army Medical Center near Denver, Colorado. We had stayed in telephone contact, but now, a year after my surgery, he arranged for me to be admitted to Fitzsimons for extensive follow-up testing and his own intensive examination.

Even before this post-surgical next meeting with Doctor Carter, however, the Lord made it abundantly and remarkably clear that He was blessedly continuing the miracle He had begun several months before at Landsthul Hospital.

While I and everyone around me had grown accustomed to my gruff and low volume voice, I was constantly frustrated by my inability to communicate with normal clarity. Even more, I was greatly saddened by my inability to sing more than a few words of any hymn. Praise God! He was very aware of my longing!

During one particularly blessed Sunday service, as the chapel congregation was offering a song of praise to the Lord, and I was earnestly croaking along, deeply longing to sing out my heart in loud and clear praise, suddenly, I felt a wonderful, normal feeling in my throat where before there had been a restraining soreness.

I immediately responded to a compelling urge to test what seemed to be some new enhanced capability. Tentatively, I did so, and then joyfully in full, loud and perfectly unrestrained voice, I found myself miraculously singing along: "To God be the glory through Jesus His Son and give Him the glory great things He has done—Praise the Lord! Praise the Lord! Let the people rejoice—"

Great things he had done, indeed. And, rejoice I did that day, and rejoice I have every time since, each time I have miraculously been thus enabled to lift up my voice to joyfully sing out His praise!!

The Lord, in His great love and infinite mercy had seen fit to do what was *impossible*. He had knit back together the surgically severed nerve that had until then greatly inhibited my larynx.

Doctor Carter, when confronted with this reality, could offer no explanation. He could only express his own amazement. But he and I both were soon to be even more profoundly amazed.

When I had admitted myself to Fitzsimons for the follow-up visit, I was immediately embarked upon a great and varied battery of what I had assumed must be every neurological test ever devised by the medical profession. This was an all day activity, and I was scheduled to meet Doctor Carter in his office the next morning.

I was anxious to see this unique, incredibly gifted surgeon who had already had such a monumentally important influence upon my life. I knocked on his office door at the appointed hour and was immediately invited to enter.

Doctor Carter greeted me with great warmth, but I could sense somehow that he was troubled. He didn't give me time to pursue my instinct, but rather confirmed it himself.

"Bob, you've got to have a look at your x-rays," he said, as he pointed to the place I was to sit, directly in front of a self-illuminated x-ray viewer. The film displayed there seemed frighteningly familiar.

"This is how your spinal column looked post-surgery a year ago," he explained, professionally. "Look right here," he pointed to the clearly visible bone plug he had taken from my hip and grafted between two vertebrae. "This is where you had the problem we fixed," he said with some just discernible hint of pride.

"Now," he continued pointing in turn  to each of the other vertabrae along the entire length of my spinal column. "These are the arthritic bone spurs I told you that would continue to give you a lot of trouble and require repeated future surgeries."

"Yes, I see them," I replied somewhat fearfully. "I remember this film from a year ago. I remember it very well."

"Wait until you see this film," he said, sounding both deeply puzzled, yet  obviously pleased and excited, as he replaced the x-ray on the viewer with another. "This is the film that was taken yesterday morning. It is unmistakably yours," he said, pointing to the same unique bone plug graft, that had been so clearly visible on the year-old film.  "Do you notice any difference between this and the earlier film?" he asked.

My mouth fell open as I indeed did notice a startling difference. Before I could speak, Tom answered his own question.

"I really can't explain this Bob," now not even trying to conceal his own perhaps unprofessional sheer amazement as he once again ran his pointing finger from vertebra to vertebra.

"Just look at this!" he proclaimed. "All of the bone spurs have totally disappeared. There isn't a single trace of your arthritic disease. With the exception of  the changes from your surgery, your entire spinal column is now perfectly normal."

I was overcome  with awe as I tried to take in the magnitude of the miracle that lay before me.

*Bless the LORD, O my soul; and all that is within me, bless His holy name! Bless the LORD, O my soul, and forget not all His benefits: Who forgives all your iniquities, Who heals all your diseases, Who redeems your life from destruction, Who crowns you with loving kindness and tender mercies, Who satisfies your mouth with good things, so that your youth is renewed like the eagle's.* (Ps 103:1-5)

## Part Two

## The Kaleidoscope

*My sheep hear My voice, and I know them, and they follow Me.—-The God of our fathers has chosen you that you should know His will, and see the Just One, and hear the voice of His mouth. For you will be His witness to all men of what you have seen and heard.*(John 10:27, Acts 22:14-15)

## Introduction

It seemed like a lifetime since I had stood in this very place, but, to my amazement, here I was again. I had just checked in to the Holiday Inn at Destin, Florida, and, in what had to have been a divine drawing, found myself making my way across the silver sand beach to the nearby surf. The sun was about to set, painting the evening sky in a panorama of indescribably elegant pastel colors.

Except for the screaming assortment of circling gulls and the skirting to and fro  sandpipers who seemed to be welcoming me back to this place after my long absence,  I found myself totally alone in the midst of all this incredible beauty.

This was to be my last business trip for the Boeing Company, I reflected nostalgically, trying to fight off a wave of sadness.

Yes, I tried to persuade myself, we were  *committed* to making *aliyah* to Israel in just a few short weeks, and there would be no turning back. I thus marveled all the more at how God had returned me to this very special place at this highly significant time.

It was here I had proposed to Donna, and it was here that I now sensed in my spirit that He had something  new and very important to share with me.

I stood by the water, just near enough so that the last remnant of an occasional incoming swell came ever so close to  lapping at my  shoes, threatening to erase their bright shine. Caught in a deepening reverie I began to pray, more accurately to *commune* with my Lord and my God.

"Abba," I beseeched the Lord God of Israel, "I praise you and I thank you for bringing me once again to this precious place. O, Lord," I questioned, "how long has it been since I was last here?"

In one of those always astounding, wonderful moments, He spoke to me in a still, quiet voice  I could "hear" in the depths of my being, a voice that I had come to know as unmistakably His.

"Thirty-three years, my son," He replied.

I was overcome by the significance of His response.

"Thirty-three years," I repeated in amazement.

"O Lord, that's how long Your Son, Yeshua walked the face of the earth.

"Abba, look at what You did with His life." Then I dared to ask, "What have You been doing with mine?"

His reply was at once immediate, clear, and unmistakably to the point. "I have been *preparing* you, My son."

I was overwhelmed by the spiritual intensity of this moment. It was too wonderful for me to bear. Reverently, I retreated from the shore and returned to the hotel where I sought to get some rest before my business meeting scheduled for early the next morning, immediately after which I was to depart for Seattle.

I didn't sleep well that night. I simply could not stop thinking about the wonder of my earlier poignant encounter with the Lord. Later, I had to struggle to stay focused during the hour-long business meeting that followed before I rushed to catch a Southern Airways connecting flight to Memphis where I would board my flight home to Seattle.

As the ancient DC-3 "Gooney Bird" lumbered along, I tried to concentrate on the Christian Ethics textbook that I held in my hands. Such was my life in those busy days of preparation, that I was now hurrying home from Destin, Florida, to the opposite corner of the country to attend a seminary class in Tacoma, Washington that evening. Still the memory of my encounter with the Lord permeated my thinking, and I simply couldn't concentrate. The enemy tried to horn in on my spiritual bliss, sowing the seeds of doubt. "Was it real?" I questioned myself silently. Then I barely whispered, "Lord, if it really was you, give me a sign."

I immediately felt deeply ashamed of myself for even daring to question the marvel of what had so recently occurred—yet? Mechanically, I turned the page of my text, again trying to focus on the task at hand. At first I could not begin to take in the significance of what my eyes perceived clearly printed on the page before me. But, then, I knew it could be nothing else but the confirmation I had just dared to seek. There in black and white, totally out of context in the chapter where it had been placed, seemingly for me alone, were the words: "Jesus walked the face of the earth for thirty-three years."

Once again, the enemy sought to destroy the moment by casting further seeds of disbelief. "Lord, if this is really you," I found myself whispering, "then give me *another* sign." I repented, shocked, and again deeply ashamed for having even *thought* with such a lack of faith in the face of such a compelling, divine visitation. But, even as I tried to mouth words of my sincere repentance, I was distracted by the loud public address system as the stewardess began to announce departure gate information for the continuing flights from Memphis.

"The flight to Boston will depart from Gate 27," she began, droning on with information of no interest whatsoever to me. Then, totally unaware of the significance of what she was about to offer and who had arranged it, presumably for my ears alone, she continued, "the flight to Seattle will depart from Gate 33."

Yes, I reflected with the grace of understanding, the Lord had been preparing me for my *aliyah* to Israel during these past thirty-three years. My spirit rejoiced within me as I was suddenly given to recall that it was thirty-three years ago I had been born again, and in that very same year, I had met and fallen in love with Donna.

I took this incredible meeting with the Lord the evening before, and this now twice-repeated confirmation as an absolute assurance that He had indeed called us home to the Land of our inheritance. Even more, I *knew* that this calling home to Israel was yet another of the several brightly colored kaleidoscope panels of His rapidly unfolding, entirely new and immediately forthcoming plan for our lives.

## Chapter One

## From Black and White to Technicolor

*John answered, saying to them all, "I indeed bap-
tize you with water; but One mightier than I is
coming, whose sandal strap I am not worthy to
loose. He will baptize you with the Holy Spirit and
with fire.* (Luke 3:16)

Pastor John Lee returned our greeting as Donna and I  wel-
comed him into our  home in Shorewood on the Shore, a suburb
of Seattle, and led him into our warm and comfortably furnished
living room. He took a seat in an overstuffed chair facing the
glowing fireplace.

"How long have you been with Boeing?" our guest began his
pastoral visit, as Donna and I took our places on an adjacent love
seat.

"It's been almost four years," I replied. "This has been such a
busy and exciting time."

"Tell me about it," Pastor Lee invited.

"I got hired when Boeing took it into their heads to get into ground-based command and control systems," I began. "They needed someone with my background to help them shape a bid for the "Peace Shield" Saudi Arabia Air Defense System. They really didn't expect to win this multi-billion dollar program against the specialists in this field, like Hughes and others, but they wanted to get their feet wet."

"Yes," he responded with recognition, "Boeing's win of this program was quite the subject of conversation around here about three years ago. It really gave a boost to the local economy. How exciting for you, Bob—to be involved in something like this!"

"They probably gave me a lot more credit than I was due, but right after the contract award I was assigned as Boeing's marketing representative to their consortium in Brussels. The idea was to design and then sell a system like Peace Shield to NATO."

"When did you get back from Brussels?" our guest asked with obvious interest.

"Just over a year ago," I responded. "Boeing was bidding on another similar program for Thailand, and they had me slated to be the Deputy Program Manager, headquartered in Bangkok."

"What happened?" our guest inquired.

"Systems Development Corporation beat us out," I replied. "Our bid came in just a bit too high, but I guess you know, that's how things go in this business."

"What have they got you doing now?"

"Let me answer that one, Pastor," Donna replied. "They have him flying all over the world. He's gone at least *half* the time."

"You don't seem to be too unhappy," our guest replied, reacting to the obvious delight in Donna's response.

"That's for sure," she explained. "I have been going with him quite often. Can you imagine, I'm actually encouraged to do this so I can be sort of a hostess for Bob when he entertains important potential customers."

"Wonderful!" he exclaimed, picking up on Donna's excitement, "But all that travel must cost you a fortune!"

"That's the neat part," Donna went on, "Boeing buys Bob a business class ticket  which, as a matter of practice, the airlines almost always upgrade to first class. I buy the cheapest economy ticket I can find, and, *of course*, the airlines upgrade me  all the way to front cabin so I can sit with my husband."

I couldn't resist joining in. "Needless to say, when we get to these places, we have to keep up the image, so we stay in all the finest places and eat in the most elegant restaurants. Honestly, pastor, I can't believe they actually *pay* me to do this."

"You two certainly have been greatly blessed by the Lord," he stated with conviction. He then got to the purpose of his visit. "Where have you been worshipping since you returned from Brussels?"

"Let me explain," I responded. "We've only been in this house a month. We moved here from a rental on Vashon Island. We'd been living there for eighteen months. We started looking to buy on the mainland when ferry travel stopped being a novelty."

"You didn't answer his question," Donna interjected. "All during our Air Force years, we were very active in the  non-denominational chapel program. Then we attended an English-speaking non-denominational Church in Brussels. The problem was,  we couldn't find a non-denominational Church on Vashon. So, since our favorite Air Force chaplains were Lutherans, we settled on a Lutheran Church."

"Do you now consider yourselves Lutheran?" our visitor inquired hopefully.

"*No*," I responded, perhaps too abruptly. "We felt comfortable in that Church, but, so far, have never really been able to subscribe to some of its liturgical approach to worship. Even after a year, a lot of this seems very new and strange to us."

"But, still, you came to our Church last Sunday?"

"Yes, we did," I replied, "and we enjoyed it very much."

"We would be so pleased if you were to join us on a regular basis," he invited warmly. "Take my word for it, the strangeness will wear off in time, and you will eventually feel like you belong."

"We will certainly give it a try," I said, as our guest rose from his seat, sensing that he had accomplished his purpose.

Then, out of the "clear blue sky," I blurted out a totally unrehearsed and not consciously considered question that I seemed to be hearing myself speak. "Tell me, Pastor, what is this business of speaking in tongues all about?"

He hesitated for a moment, trying to frame an appropriate response. "Let's talk about that later," he said finally, shaking our hands and then heading for the door.

"What was that all about?" Donna asked, quite puzzled as our guest drove off.

"Honestly, Sweetheart," I responded, not even trying to conceal my own perplexity, "I haven't got the faintest idea."


Pastor John Lee had been very right in his prediction. We soon became quite comfortable in our new Church surroundings, although we continued to refuse to consider ourselves denominationally Lutheran. Even so, I soon found myself appointed as a member of the Church board, and not long after, invited to deliver a lay sermon one Sunday. Despite all this, I held firm to one area of resistance: I flatly refused to join any of the several midweek fellowship program home groups that our pastor strongly endorsed. Donna was much more inclined to give one of these groups a try, and she, in her own well-practiced way, continued to "work her way" in wearing down my resistance. In the meantime, she had honored my wishes and politely declined invitations from two of these groups for us to meet with them.

I was thus more than a little surprised one particular Sunday, when we found ourselves sitting in a pew directly behind Bill and Caroline Ebright, a lovely staunchly Lutheran couple, then in their sixties, who had been pillars of this Church for many years. Just as the service was about to begin, Caroline turned around suddenly and quite matter-of-factly invited Donna: "Our home group will be meeting Wednesday evening at seven o'clock. Would you and Bob like to join us?"

Later, Donna, fully aware of my strong feelings to the contrary, and up to now, her out-of-hand rejection of other such invitations, was unable to explain, even to herself, her unhesitatingly excited response. "Yes, Caroline, we would *love* to!"

When we entered the Ebright residence the next Wednesday evening, my initial resistance to having been "dragged along" to this unfamiliar kind of gathering quickly gave way to the overpowering sense of spirituality and warmth that permeated the place.

There was something greater and more compelling than just the obviously genuine Christian fellowship in this otherwise unpretentious home. Deep within my spirit I sensed the presence of "someone" rather than "something." For the first time in my walk of over thirty years, I felt the incredible, magnificent and very personal presence of God in this place. Inexplicably, I felt a great outpouring of love for these now suddenly transformed "brothers and sisters" who had, up to this moment, been little more than strangers. Yet, for me, personally, I *knew* there was still something terribly missing. Even as I felt myself being bathed in their genuine love, I somehow understood that this wonderful outpouring flowed from the very throne of God. Suddenly, my deep perplexity gave way to a supernatural understanding. *They* were connected to something that *I* was not. Silently, from the depths of my being, I cried out, "Help me, O

Lord!" Then, in the very next instant, I found myself looking into the somehow understanding eyes of my host, Bill Ebright.

"Bill," I blurted out without any forethought whatsoever, "what is this business of speaking in other tongues?"

Even today, many years later, I continue to marvel at the incredible significance of this question, the answer, and aftermath of which totally revamped our walk with the Lord as it dramatically redirected the pathways of our lives. How utterly amazing it was that God had led us quite pointedly to the one "closet" charismatic home group from the several in our quite staid, traditional and otherwise non-charismatic Lutheran Church.

Bill responded as if he had been anticipating my question. He withdrew a book from a nearby, crowded shelf and handed it to me. "For starters," he smiled knowingly, "read this. Let me know when you're finished, and if you have any questions. Then, we'll go on from there."

Donna and I had both been smitten by the Holy Spirit that first evening with the Ebrights, but we hadn't even begun to understand the profound significance of what the Lord had apparently determined to work in our lives.

During the next few days, we both "consumed" John Sherrill's foundational work *They Speak With Other Tongues*. The author, we learned had been a skeptic as far as miracles were concerned. Then the magazine he worked for sent him to investigate a strange biblical event that was cropping up across the country: the phenomenon of speaking in tongues. His search led him on an adventure that was to have profound personal results. His book was a wonderful, amazing account of how he had sought to investigate, then discredit the exploding Charismatic Renewal of the early 1960's, but instead, had himself received the baptism of the Holy Spirit.

Bill and Caroline greeted us with hugs the next Wednesday

evening. As we stepped inside, we once again felt the wonderful and pervasive presence of the Holy Spirit. I returned John Sherrill's wonderful book handing it to Bill. I struggled to find just the right words, but before I could offer our great thanks, I sensed their complete understanding. "What's next?" I asked with growing excitement and anticipation.

I have long understood that God uses certain people of His creation to serve as vessels through which to communicate His will and way to others. It was on this second evening with the Ebrights that we were introduced to such a chosen vessel who was to have a tremendous impact upon both of our lives.

Bill returned John Sherrill's book to its place on the crowded shelf and withdrew another. "This is Dennis Bennett's *Nine O'Clock in the Morning*," he said knowingly, as he handed over his selection. Dennis Bennett, we were soon to learn, was an Episcopal priest who had been the pastor of a huge and thriving congregation in Southern California. He had been very highly regarded by the hierarchy of his Church and was about to be made a bishop. As it turned out, the Holy Spirit had other plans for this very special vessel. Dennis Bennett, it seems, had become aware that two young couples in his congregation had experienced what was reportedly some strange encounter with the Holy Spirit. He thus determined to personally investigate the matter and to correct any error in their understanding. Instead, Dennis Bennett received the baptism of the Holy Spirit and found himself incredibly transformed and renewed as he cried out his thanksgiving in a language he himself did not understand.

The next Sunday, when Dennis Bennett announced to his congregation that he had experienced this new outpouring of God's spirit, all hope for his imminent elevation to bishop was vanquished forthwith. Instead, he was banished to a tiny, decrepit, and failing Church in Ballard, Washington, a northern suburb of Seattle. Even so, Dennis Bennett was soon to become the recognized founder and leader of the worldwide Second Pentecostal revival, which came to be universally known as the "Charismatic Renewal." And, his once nearly defunct Church was quickly transformed into the geographic center from which emanated this amazing spiritual renewal that impacted untold millions of Christians around the world.

Bill Ebright, we were to learn during the following week as we both hungrily poured over and digested this latest, incredible, borrowed book, was, at least in this respect, a master of understatement. This book was far more than just a *blessing* to us. It was a critical building block in what we both had only begun to suspect was a major overhaul and redirection of our walk with the Lord. The following Wednesday the ongoing great blessing of Dennis Bennett's writings continued to pour forth upon our lives, this time in the form of *The Holy Spirit and You*, the monumental "text book" of the Charismatic Renewal its founder had co-authored with his wife Rita. Two weeks later, when we had both finished and thoroughly taken in this major work, we knew that we were on the brink of a major working of the Lord in our lives. It was just a few days before Christmas, and Bill had yet another very special gift for us. It was then that he blessed us with the third of the three Dennis Bennett works that had already shaken the worldwide Church. Its title spoke for itself: *How to Pray for the Release of the Holy Spirit.*

Donna was working the day shift the following Saturday, so I had our house all to myself. With my new treasure in hand, I retreated to our downstairs den. I started a fire in the fireplace, sat down in my favorite lounge chair and began to read Dennis Bennett's third, and for me, most fateful offering.

Slowly I read, then reread each page, trying to make certain that I missed nothing of importance along the way. So lost was I in my reading that I lost track of time, and there, turning the page,

I found myself confronted with Chapter 9 "Prayer for Baptism in the Holy Spirit."

I carefully examined all that I had so far read. *Yes,* I had once again declared my unshakable and complete acceptance of Jesus Christ as my Savior and Lord. *Yes,* once again I had carefully and completely repented for all of my sins that I struggled to bring to mind, desperately trying to leave none unspoken and delivered thus to His throne where they might be forgiven and forever forgotten. *Yes,* I was hungry, I was seeking, and I read on, repeating the words of the most earnestly heartfelt prayer I have ever uttered:

> Father, I claim the protection of the blood of Jesus over me. I ask You to send your angels to stand around me and drive away any spirit of fear, doubt or confusion. Holy Spirit, I ask you for a new Pentecost. Praise You Father, I receive this wonderful gift of spiritual renewal that you have for me. Father, please, in your mercy and in your grace, please baptize me in the Holy Spirit. Thank You Father! I receive! I accept the new language You have given me. Yes, Lord, in the name of Jesus, help me to release it.

In the very next instant, I found myself in the midst of the most overwhelming and utterly astounding experience of my life! The Creator of the universe had seen fit to answer my heartfelt plea and to answer it abundantly. I was on my knees, crying out to God in some new Middle Eastern-sounding language I could not understand. I whispered these strange words, then spoke them in a normal voice, then shouted them out! I was out of control, totally caught up in an intensely, most profound spiritual ecstasy, the likes of which I had never before imagined possible! I found myself pleading with God at some lingering conscious level of

my soul not to let this incredible happening end. And He immediately answered even this prayer for more and more as, to my
utterly complete and indescribable happiness, this, my first praying in the Spirit, continued to pour forth from the depth of my
being in a seemingly unending explosion of pure, unrestrained
and overwhelming joy! It was as if everything spiritual in my life
had suddenly gone from drab black and white to glorious tech-
nicolor. I was in a state of absolute peace. I had lost track of time
and could only estimate that this first outpouring of the Spirit had
gone on for about a half hour. I found myself stretched out on
the couch in front of the fire, still winding down from the amazing bliss of my experience.

"Hi Sweetheart!" Donna called me from my lingering reverie
as she, in her wonderful, full-of-life-way, bounced into the den.

"You'll never guess what happened to me just now," I
responded to her greeting, trying to find some way to explain my
genuinely indescribable experience. I couldn't contain my
incredible joy and excitement. I nearly shouted: "I've been baptized with the Holy Spirit!!"

"Ohh," she responded matter-of-factly, as if I had just reported on some everyday household experience, her voice echoing
not even a hint of my own potpourri of emotion. "That's nice."

Two days following this most momentous experience in my
life, Donna and I were driving from Seattle to Phoenix where we
were to spend the upcoming Christmas week with Cindy and
Julie. While I had been trying to come to grips with my still very
new and incredible spiritual renewal, one major "problem" kept
crowding in to dampen my indescribable joy. How, I asked
myself again and again, how can I go through the rest of my life
so greatly blessed without Donna actively sharing this new experience. For the first time, I understood the stilted-sounding term
"unequally yoked" and it literally made me tremble. My beloved

wife and I had up to now, shared a close spiritual commonality, a closeness which was a very foundation of our relationship and family. Now, suddenly, as blessed as I had just remarkably become, I felt strangely disconnected from my spiritual partner for life. I looked for a way around this barrier, but the reality of it kept coming back: we no longer had an unrestricted basis for sharing. It was as if we were suddenly living in different spiritual dimensions.

During our drive from Seattle, we exchanged only a few non-committal surface comments about my *experience*, both of us deliberately avoiding the subject, as the growing distance between us began to be almost palpable. Part of this avoidance on my part was my hesitation to "try out" my prayer language again, just to test the continuing reality of its existence. Now, however, as we stopped for the night at a small motel just beyond the Oregon border, I felt a deep and compelling need to validate what had happened to so abruptly change my life just two days earlier. How could I cry out to the Lord in tongues, I pondered, when there was no way for me to be physically alone. Then, as we entered our room for the night, a means for satisfying my growing need became apparent. "Sweetheart, I think I'll take a nice hot shower before dinner, if you don't mind," I announced as I determined that the stall shower at one end of the room would make a convenient prayer closet.

"Sounds like a great idea. I'll take one after you," she responded.

I could hardly wait to turn the water up to full volume, the rushing sound of which I felt certain would mask the prayerful outcry that had been welling up in me for the past two days. "O God," I thought fearfully as I opened my mouth, "what if—but the words of my new language rushed out, first in a normal speaking volume, then, in just moments, I found myself actually wailing without restraint in these strange Middle-Eastern-sounding words.

It was indescribably wonderful. I lost track of time and space as I wailed on, lifted out of my immediate surroundings transported to some incredible new spiritual dimension. Then, just as suddenly as it had begun, my outpouring was finished. I turned off the water and stepped out of the shower.

Donna was sitting in a nearby chair as I dried myself. "That was really something else!" she exclaimed. Knowing that I had been "discovered," I was filled with a sinking feeling, as I desperately looked for a way to explain. Then it became apparent that no explanation was necessary, after all. "You sounded like you were calling the people to prayer," she said knowingly and understandingly as tears began to run down her cheeks. "It was wonderful, divine—I want this too, so badly." We both then knew that God would make a way for us to share in this incredible gift, we just didn't know when or how. We weren't to be long delayed or in any way disappointed.

A few weeks later, I was required to attend some business meetings in Seoul, Korea. Donna declined to come along, electing instead to recover from what had been a wonderful yet tiring holiday visit with the girls.

It was Sunday evening, and I had just returned to my room at the Seoul Hilton after having experienced the most wonderful Church service of my life. A friend had earlier suggested that I attend Paul Yongi Cho's Yoido Full Gospel Church next time I got to Seoul, and, to my absolute wonder and delight, I had just done so.

By 1981, the Yoido Full Gospel Church had reached a membership of 200,000 and had become the largest Church in the world. It has maintained that distinction ever since, and by 1990, it had peaked with over 700,000 members. Even with a main sanctuary that seats over 25,000 people, several services are required here each Sunday as well as in its twelve, closed circuit television connected satellite Churches to accommodate this huge congregation. What a thrill it was for me to attend one of the services in the main sanctuary this particular Sunday. Pastor Cho's sermon had been remarkable enough, but when the 25,000 worshipers began to collectively "pray in the Spirit," and I had spontaneously joined in this outpouring, it was an experience I shall never forget.

> *And I heard, as it were, the voice of a great multitude, as the sound of many waters and as the sound of mighty thunderings, saying, "Alleluia! For the Lord God Omnipotent reigns!* (Rev 19:6)

Now back in my hotel room, I felt the sudden need to pray, and I fell on my knees beside the bed. "O Lord!" I cried out an even more immediate version of the prayer I had often been praying since my own recent spiritual renewal. "Please, Dear Lord, in your mercy and in your grace, visit Donna *this very moment.* Bestow upon her your indescribable gift of baptism with the Holy Spirit so that we might be equally yoked with you in our walk together." Then, in one of those wonderful, undeniable moments, I heard His still quiet voice in response, "Call her on the phone, *right now,* my son." Without hesitation, I reached for the nearby phone and dialed our number in Seattle. "Hi Sweetheart!" I greeted her, feeling even more than the usual rush of love and joy at the sound of her voice. But even before I could say another word....

"Just now, Darling, just now," she cried out joyfully, "while I was sitting up in bed praying, suddenly I was—" She paused momentarily, then confirmed her own amazed confirmation. "Yes," she proclaimed, "I was baptized in the Holy Spirit and I began speaking in tongues!"

I was beside myself with joy! Once again, God had immediately and completely answered my prayer.

"My prayer language is a sort of Hawaiian sounding thing," she continued excitedly.


Our spiritual lives immediately began to flourish as they had never before. We were on an incredible "trip" with the Lord. We could literally feel our growth in Him: it was palpable. Our spiritual perceptions quickly began to change as did our growing need for a more free form of worship than we could find in our traditional Lutheran Church. Nevertheless, we were reluctant to leave this delightful congregation, especially Pastor Lee, and of course Bill, Caroline and the other dear brothers and sisters in our home group whom we had come to dearly love and to whom we owed so much.

Thus, we found a solution by attending the Sunday evening service at nearby Des Moines Assembly of God Church. What a blessing our two Churches became. Between them, they met our every need, and we were utterly content in Him as we continued to marvel at our own ongoing spiritual transformation.

For me, only one thing was still missing. By nature, Donna is a very private person, sometimes even with me. Even so, despite my persistent suggestions, she had not yet felt comfortable praying with me in the spirit, and I genuinely hungered to hear her new language and to pray with her in this new, very different, yet incredibly fulfilling way. Since I knew that the Lord would, according to his timing, eventually bring to pass this very special kind of sharing with Donna, I backed off and waited as patiently as I could. Praise the Lord! I didn't have long to wait.

Hardly a week passed that we didn't eat dinner out at our favorite neighborhood Mexican restaurant. One midweek evening, about a month after my return from Korea, Donna and I were enjoying such an evening out. It was still very early evening when we finished eating, and it was one of those extremely rare picture-post-card "perfect" Seattle days. The sun was shining warmly, and, quite uncharacteristically, there wasn't a cloud in the sky.

"How about a walk along the beach at Salt Water State Park," I suggested spontaneously. Donna quickly agreed. This waterfront park was an especially lovely place for a walk, and very near where we lived.

Thus we soon found ourselves arm in arm, strolling along the pebbly shore of Puget Sound, absorbed in one another and in the lovely surroundings the Lord had chosen for what was to be a very memorable occasion. We were deep in conversation and lost track of how far we had walked until we realized we were at the extreme northern boundary of the park. There wasn't another soul anywhere to be seen;  thus we had this lovely, almost enchanted place to ourselves. Moved by the Holy Spirit, I walked to the edge of the beach, and facing the incredible sunset that had just begun to color the sky, I raised my hands to the Lord and began to pray.

Within a few moments, I felt Donna's presence beside me, and I caught a glimpse of her upraised hands as she joined me in prayer, praising the Lord in the unique language she  had been miraculously given.

My joy was now complete and, evidently, so was hers. On and on we prayed, and when we finished, the sun had finally disappeared behind the magnificent snowcapped Olympic Mountains on the far side of the water. We embraced but were soon distracted by the very nearby, loud and lovely cooing sound of two birds. We had been standing under the end of a fallen tree limb that extended all the way to the water's edge. Instinctively, we both looked directly above where we stood, and there, literally close enough to reach out and touch, no more than three feet from our heads, were a pair of beautiful doves. Like us, they were snuggled close together, and we surmised, also like us, they were praising the Lord in their own very special way.

Beyond the obvious spiritual implications of this truly remarkable visitation was the fact that doves are extremely rare in this part of western Washington, where such a sighting as the one we had just experienced would have been a remarkable phenomenon for even the most diligent professional bird watcher.

> *When He had been baptized, Jesus came up immediately from the water; and behold, the heavens were opened to Him, and He saw the Spirit of God descending like a dove and alighting upon Him.* (Matt 3:16)

## Chapter Two

## A Call to "Faith"

*"Therefore prepare yourself and arise, and speak to them all that I command you."—- And He opened their understanding, that they might comprehend the Scriptures.* (Jer 1:17a, Luke 24:45)

The enormous and continuing success of the Boeing Company, I believe, can in a great way be attributed to its seemingly insatiable appetite to equip itself with the very best technical and intellectual minds available. The company almost exclusively hires those with advanced degrees, and it is not uncommon for members of the staff to hold multiple doctorates. Only on those very rare occasions when special skills and experience are specifically needed, will they hire those, such as me at that time, with a non-technical Bachelor of Arts.

Daniel S. Joseph was just such an amazingly brilliant intellectual. He also happened to be a Messianic Jew, and he had quickly become my best and closest company friend and confidant.

Daniel holds a doctorate in engineering with a specialty in computer-controlled, artificial human limb design. He completed all academic requirements for his second doctorate in medicine to better equip himself to pursue his first  high tech prosthesis design passion. However, as is often the case, he was now working "out of his field" as a staff systems engineer on various complex new command and control system projects. Daniel also had, more within my realm of understanding,  a remarkable gift of prophecy from the Lord which manifested itself in clear and highly detailed visions, the content of which he often shared with me during our daily coffee breaks together.

While there may have been others, during our several years together, Daniel only shared two such visions in which I was the principal  subject.  I had initially dismissed both of these as too far out to be given any credence whatsoever. The first of Daniel's visions he shared with me in late January 1991, while I was still spiritually "boiling over" in the aftermath of my recent spiritual renewal.

Daniel, who had  himself been "Spirit-filled" for many years, was an enormous blessing to me in his always ready willingness to quietly absorb the frequent, excited testimonies of my continuing spiritual "discoveries," all of which he well understood from long, personal experience. As was his way, Daniel got right to the point one day when he began our conversation with  what seemed to me to be a completely off the wall question:  "What seminary do you want to attend, Bob?  I really think Fuller would be a good choice. You know they have an extension in Seattle."

I was shocked and totally unprepared for what I had just heard. I responded with immediate disbelief: "You must have me confused with someone else. Never in my wildest imagination have I thought about attending seminary. Daniel, I am fifty-six years old, in the midst of a wonderful second career—you must be out of your mind!"

My very dear, highly intellectual friend smiled knowingly, "Fuller may not be the best choice after all," he said. "They *are* quite liberal, and I believe they are quite expensive. We really need to pray about this."

"And just when is all this supposed to happen?" I responded sarcastically in the face of his persistence, hoping to shut him off.

"You can look for a clear seminary call in a few months," he replied.

The Lord indeed, quietly and step by step, confirmed to me the vision He had given Daniel. First, He gradually transformed what had initially seemed outrageous, into the beginning of my tacit acceptance. Then, seamlessly, He grew my tacit acceptance into my *full*, yet still somewhat reluctant, recognition that He was doing something very special and very different in my life. Then, to make His point inescapably clear, He blotted out every bit of my lingering reluctance in the wake of what very quickly became a growing, then all-consuming passion. By, early April, I *knew* that Daniel's word for me had flowed right from the heart of the Lord. It wasn't a question anymore of *if* I should attend seminary; it had become an urgency and only a matter of *where* and *when*.

Donna, Daniel, Sheryl (Daniel's lovely spirit filled wife) and I made this "where and when" the subject of frequent prayer. The answer came through Donna while I was on a business trip to Washington, D.C.

There are several Christian radio stations in the Seattle area; two of them were Donna's favorites she had pre-selected on her car radio. She often went from one to the other as she drove, listening to which ever caught her attention. On this particular occasion, the Lord had something very special for us both as she randomly selected one of the stations while she drove to work at a local hospital where she was employed. It seemed that this station had been doing a one time series of interviews with the presidents of the several local seminaries. And, at this very moment, Donna was listening to such a conversation between the interviewer and the Reverend Doctor R.H. Redal, President and founder of Faith Seminary in Tacoma, Washington.

Donna was very anxious to share her experience when she reached me by phone that evening in my Washington, D.C. hotel room. "I just *know* they are everything we have been praying for," she excitedly reported as she listed each of Faith Seminary's key features. "They are very conservative; have a non-denominational faculty, including, can you believe it, Pentecostals; and they teach the inerrancy of Scripture!"

"This *does* sound interesting," I replied, "but do they take part-time students, and when could I get started?"

"Yes," Donna replied, still bubbling over, "they *do* take part-time students and the next quarter starts in only three weeks. If you want me to, I'll give them a call tomorrow morning and get all the details."

"By all means, do!" I replied, not even trying to mask my own growing excitement as I sensed, even then, the Lord showing me: "This is the place I have chosen for you."

Although I had made every effort *not* to do so, I could scarcely think of anything else but my imminent initiation as a graduate student, even though at this moment I was challenged by a high level business meeting in Ottawa to where I had just traveled with one of our senior executives.

Not only had I been fighting back waves of self-doubt about my academic ability to operate at this level of intellectual challenge "at my age," but I also came under increasing attack from the enemy regarding my spiritual qualifications for taking this bold step into the ministry. More and more, the memories of my numerous, sinful shortcomings flooded accusingly into my consciousness, making me all the more convinced that I was by no means worthy of such a high calling. Even while I had carried on a perfunctory conversation with my senior associate during the long flight from Seattle to Ottawa, this laundry list of my inadequacies for the ministry or anything associated with it kept disquietingly passing in review before my inner eye.

Now, after we landed at Ottawa International Airport and were taking a taxi to our downtown hotel, it finally occurred to me that I might find some solace from my unnerving state of mind in prayer. "O, Lord," I beseeched in the silent sanctuary of my mind, "in the name of Jesus, I ask for confirmation that *you* have called me to seminary despite all of my own great unworthiness."

Immediately, I heard Him answer me in what had now become an increasingly familiar, still quiet voice. "Hurry, my son, look to your left! *Hurry*, don't miss what I have for you!" I obeyed. Turning abruptly in my seat, I looked to the left where I instantly noted we were just passing the First Baptist Church of Ottawa. On the sidewalk, right in front of the Church, there was a marquee showing the schedule of events for the upcoming Sunday. Included was the title of the sermon that would be preached, a title that in itself carried a profound message for me personally from the very heart of God to my own. It was very difficult for me to choke back my tears as I read the title: "There Are No Stains on the Pages of Tomorrow."

Later, after we arrived at the hotel and checked in, my associate and I agreed to meet for dinner at a nearby, highly recommended restaurant. I had only one lingering encumbrance. It seems I had been wearing a brand-new pair of expensive Italian black loafers which, to my great chagrin, had taken a very serious toll on my left big toe. I was horrified when, at the appointed hour, as I tried to put my left shoe back on, there was no physical possibility for me to do so. My big toe was swollen to nearly twice its normal size and it was throbbing painfully, offering its strong protest as I tried to cram it into its previous, now far too small prison.

At this point in my spiritual walk, operating in the spiritual gifts was still very new to my experience. Yet, what else was there to do? Here I had a dinner engagement with a person who could and probably would very seriously impact my future career with the Boeing Company, to say nothing about the important business meeting where I was expected to "perform" the following morning. As it stood, I reasoned, I would have difficulty satisfying either of these important requirements with a shoeless left foot.

"Okay, Lord," I cried out, not *really* believing, yet doing my best to do so as I sat on the side of the bed staring at my badly swollen and painfully afflicted left foot. "In the name of Jesus, I claim a complete healing for my left big toe."

No sooner had I said "Amen" than before my very eyes I watched, incredulously as my toe slowly receded to its normal size, the redness entirely disappearing and the pain replaced by a healthy, warm tingling.

I sang a series a praise songs of thanksgiving as I finished dressing and hurried to meet my companion for dinner.


Typically, it was raining that first evening when I arrived at the Faith Seminary campus, having driven the forty-five minutes from Seattle after work for the first session of my inaugural graduate level class. I was, frankly, terrified, deeply mindful of the fact that it had been thirty-five years since I had set foot in a college class room.

"Can I hack this?" I whispered to both myself and the Lord as I stepped out of my car and was immediately drawn to the nearby lawn where a huge wooden cross was planted and towered over the landscape. Ignoring the rain that was busily soaking my Boeing marketer "uniform of the day," an unprotected, tailor-made, three-piece business suit, I walked to the base of the cross and felt compelled to literally embrace it as I prayed for special favor for this new undertaking. From that very first evening, I never failed to pause for a moment here, at the foot of this wonderful cross, to seek His favor for what lay ahead.

Praise God for answered prayer. My time at Faith Seminary was unquestionably the most edifying experience of my life. I virtually consumed the many volumes of assigned reading, relished in the lectures and hungered for more and yet more. The entire experience was anointed—simply wonderful!

"What next?" I wondered as Doctor Jim Roane, an Assembly of God faculty member, announced to the soon to be graduates at the end of our final class together: "I have a word from the Lord for each of you graduates, just in case you would like to know what He has in mind for you."

Because I was about to receive only an interim one-year "Diploma in Christian Studies," I felt this word for me was somehow premature, since I would be spending the next year finishing my Master of Christian Ministries. I was, as usual in matters like this, mistaken.

Doctor Roane addressed us individually, in turn, announcing the specific call God had on each of our lives. Without exception, each of the graduates were called to be pastors—that is, until it came to me.

"Bob," Doctor Roane intoned, "you are to be a Christian businessman." I was profoundly and deeply disappointed, even flabbergasted. I could hardly wait to challenge this unseemly pronouncement.

"Surely, Doctor Roane," I almost shouted as I intercepted my favorite professor after class, "you must be mistaken—I *already am* a Christian businessman! Even though I will primarily be a missionary, I want to *preach*! Isn't that why people are called to seminary?"

He put a comforting arm around my shoulder. "Bob, *trust* the Lord. He has something very special for you, very special indeed. It *isn't* a pulpit. Wait on Him."

# Chapter Three

## Embracing My Jewish Heritage  in  a House of Joy (*Beth  Simcha*)

I would imagine even the best of marriages has at least one recurrent bone of contention between its two participants. Certainly, Donna and I are no exception. Our one significant difference in perspective manifested itself  one star filled night, right after she had agreed to be my wife and I  had then hesitatingly "confessed" my ethnic Jewishness as if it were a major negative and a threat to our just beginning relationship.

From the moment I discovered my family secret, I had increasingly grown to think being Jewish was anything but a positive circumstance. Like Esau, my biblical  cousin  many  generations removed, I would not only have sold my birthright for a bowl of lentil stew,  I would not have hesitated for even a moment to give it away unconditionally to any taker. Like my father and his father before him, I  had diligently sought to suppress even the slightest hint of my true heritage, not only from the predominately Gentile world in which I lived,  where I sought to be  totally absorbed and  accepted, but also, perhaps even more poignantly,  I had left no stone unturned to suppress this painful reality even from myself.

Donna, on the other hand, from the moment of my revelation, to my continuing amazement, had inexplicably reacted most positively, beginning with her excitement and joy that she was, by taking up with me, about to be "married into the covenant."

At first, I had viewed her surprising reaction with relief and thanksgiving. However, with the passing of years, as she not only continued to persist in frequently reminding me of my Jewish heritage, but with ever-increasing insistence urged me to embrace it, my initial relief and thanksgiving grew into my side of what became a sort of running, but mutually accepted feud. Donna never missed a chance to bring up the subject in a variety of clever, seemingly normal, conversational ways. She rose to every opportunity and cue, those of her own manufacture and, even better, those that just happened to come along. For example, our ritual of reading the Sunday newspaper together provided predictable and fertile ground for her continuing passion. "Oh," she would comment excitedly, announcing what she had just read: "Synagogue [one of many] is having an Israeli art exhibit next week. Wouldn't it be nice to go??" To which, as if we were having such a conversation for the first time, I would reply something like, "No, I'm not interested, but by all means, feel free to go by yourself." Albeit she never went to any of these Jewish places or events by herself, she, praise the Lord, and to her great credit, never stopped suggesting that we should do so together.

Surely, it was the Lord who put the feature article about Messianic Judaism before her seeking eyes one Sunday morning, a few weeks after I had begun my first quarter at Faith Seminary. Try as she did, she couldn't contain herself.

"Ohhh, Sweetheart," she began, "did you know there was a movement of Jews who believe in Jesus right here in the Seattle area? There are even several congregations. Isn't that interesting?"

I simply couldn't help myself; I *was* interested, but I certainly *wasn't* about to admit it. "Hmmm," I replied, "I suppose it's possible for some Jews to be saved; after all, look at me—although, it does sound a bit cultic."

Even this minor acknowledgment, Donna took to be a "chink in my heretofore unpenetrated armor." Wisely, though, she changed the subject until our next weekly sharing of the Sunday paper.

"Myyy," she interjected right on cue the following Sunday, trying to seem surprised by the advertisement she had diligently scoured the religious section to find.

"There is a Messianic congregation called 'Beth Simcha' in Federal Way. It meets every Saturday morning at eleven. Wouldn't it be *fun* to check this out??"

Even to this day, from the incredibly wonderful perspective of being a citizen of the State of Israel, I marvel at my response that Sunday morning. Even though I strenuously rebelled at the idea of giving up Saturday, my one free day of the week, to yet another Church-oriented activity, all at once, I found myself finally giving up under the pressure of Donna's relentless campaign. Yes, somewhere deep down within the depths of my being I *really* was interested! Certainly, this was the Holy Spirit's very special way of moving me along in fulfillment of God's amazing and wonderful plan for my life.

I heard myself saying, "Okay, Sweetheart; find out where they meet and we'll give it a try next Saturday."


Our conversation during the forty-five minute drive south to Federal Way was mostly perfunctory. Donna hesitated to put in jeopardy what to her was a major victory. And I was deeply lost in thought, struggling with a potpourri of mostly conflicting sets of emotion: anticipation and fear; longing and rejection; sadness and joy.

"Turn left here," Donna directed,  calling me back to the moment. "According to the map,  it  should be right around the corner in the next block."

Donna spoke first as we shared our first glimpse of the large Four Square Gospel Church that each Saturday rented its facilities to Congregation Beth Simcha. "Look at that parking lot!" she exclaimed. "There must be over one hundred cars—it looks full!"

We were both greatly surprised by the apparently large size of the congregation, having assumed that there could only be a very few such "born again"  Jews who might be inclined to meet together. Now, as I took the last available parking place in the very large lot, I looked at my watch and noted that we were fifteen minutes early, and there were already several other cars behind us that would now have to park along the street,  a bit farther away from the sanctuary.

My sense of anticipation  and excitement grew; my spirit quickened as we stepped out of the car and started to walk, arm in arm,  towards the entrance of the quite plain,  yet lovely Church. Filled with peace, I found myself yielding to a sense that something very important was about to happen—something life changing in its significance.

Then I saw it. My heart started to race, pounding in my chest. My spirit soared on wings of eagles! I was filled with a strange sense of wonder and overwhelming joy! There,  planted in the lovely, lush green lawn in front of the Church, was a simple wrought-iron Star of David. My eyes darted back and forth from this symbol of my long- suppressed, ethnic heritage to the plain Christian cross that  rose from the top of the sanctuary. I felt Donna gently pulling at my arm, leading me along to some certain and wonderful destiny that  was soon to be fulfilled.

"Shabbat Shalom!" a delightful, Holy Spirit filled  sister greeted us exuberantly  as we stepped inside the Church. "My name's

Rosie," she said, introducing herself. "Welcome to Beth Simcha!" she exclaimed, as she gave me a tremendously warm "bear hug" greeting. "Shabbat Shalom, Rosie!" I returned her words, using the Hebrew greeting for the first time, only suspecting what it meant. Then I found myself saying sincerely, "We're Bob and Donna Fischer. It's *good* to be here!"

Donna was on my arm, close enough that I was wonderfully aware that we were indeed one flesh, a Gentile and a Jew, a "one new man" couple joined together for some important purpose that was far beyond my understanding of the moment. And then, in a flash, the reality of my entire spiritual being came into a new, sharp focus.

As I scanned the already crowded, nearly full, large sanctuary for some available seats, my eyes fell upon the simple wooden pulpit. It was covered with a blue-colored altar cloth, upon which was emblazoned a white Star of David. As I looked up from the star to a large Christian cross mounted on the wall behind the pulpit, the incredible significance—the wonderful reality of the moment fell upon me and I began to weep uncontrollably. For the first time in my life I understood precisely *who* and *what* I was, the person God had created me to be, and I rejoiced in this discovery! I was a *Jew* who by His grace had been saved by the shed blood of my Messiah, Jesus Christ, who, I was later to know more intimately as Yeshua. Never will I stop praising Him for that wonderful moment and all that was to follow in this, my new walk as a  self- acknowledged and self-appreciated Messianic Jew.

And so it evolved that we were now attending *three* Churches: Beth Simcha on Saturdays, St. Paul's of Shorewood on Sunday mornings, and Des Moines Assembly on Sunday evenings, all of this, while I was attending seminary full-time and pursuing a very busy and challenging marketing career with Boeing. Sadly, we concluded, something had to go. There just wasn't time in our busy schedule for us to attend more than one Church. We prayed about it, seeking guidance, and the Lord answered us during the next Shabbat service at Beth Simcha.

Our new pastor, Frank Stiller, was very closely led by the Holy Spirit, and he not infrequently stopped in the middle of delivering a message to obediently take off in some new, entirely different direction. On this particular Shabbat, Frank found himself suddenly led to share a vision from the Lord he had just received. "There is a train," he began. "It is a train from the Lord, and it is going to make a brief stop here in our station at Beth Simcha. The Lord is saying, 'Come all of you who want to get on board *my* train. This is *your* opportunity to make a decision for change—a decision to belong to this, *my* congregation!'" With that, Frank concluded, calling all to come forward who desired to get aboard this "train from the Lord." Donna and I knew that the Lord had spoken to us, as we arm in arm, joyfully went to the altar to assume our places in this very special congregation to which we knew with certainty we had been called.

So, it was with both resolve and heavy hearts that we met separately during the following week with the other two beloved pastors in our lives to explain our situation. Both expressed their understanding and genuinely shared our excitement about this new movement in our lives that was calling me back to my Jewish roots. We felt so greatly blessed as they prayed for us and fully supported our decision.

As we pulled away from the parking lot of Des Moines Assembly on what was to be our last Sunday evening service there and began to drive the five miles to our home, we both felt a great sense of change punctuated by a strange blend of sadness and joy.

"I sure hope we are doing the right thing," I said, as my eyes began to well up with tears. "I am really going to miss these dear people."

"No more than I," Donna responded with equal sadness, as she opened the sun roof for us to better enjoy the rare and lovely rain-free day. "We just have to trust the Lord that this is what He has for us."

As the sun roof locked into its open position, Donna "happened" to look up into the sky immediately above us. "Dear God!" she exclaimed in wonder. "What does that cloud look like to you?" she continued, calling my attention to this singular, very sharply defined, puffy, white presence.

"Incredible!" I responded excitedly after looking up, confirming the obvious. "It is an absolutely perfect dove with outstretched wings! How very special!"

How very special indeed! We had already noted that there wasn't another cloud to be seen anywhere, just this singular clearly defined sculpture I could only believe was carved by the hand of God just for the two of us. To our continuing utter amazement, our "dove" stayed in clear sight, immediately above our sun roof as it followed us for the entire five miles, all the way to our driveway.

"Let me run and get the camera!" I exclaimed. We were momentarily distracted as Donna activated and opened the electronic gate that protected our driveway. As I exited the car, only moments later, I looked up again to note with sadness that our heavenly visitor had suddenly disappeared without leaving a hint of the lovely and amazing presence that had been such a lingering blessing and confirmation to us both.

## Chapter Four

## Daniel's Second Vision

*Behold, I send an Angel before you to keep you in
the way and to bring you into the place which I
have prepared.* (Exod 23:20)

In November 1991, when I was well into my second academic quarter at Faith Seminary, I was already excitedly looking ahead to a mission filled summer before my classes were to resume the following September.

I therefore wasn't at all surprised when Daniel told me about the second vision concerning me he had received from the Lord. In fact, I took it as a clear confirmation of a plan I had already begun to coordinate with Issachar Frontier Missions in nearby Lynnwood. I had been introduced to Frontier, a well-known mission-oriented ministry, by Dr. Ray Arnold, my missions professor.

Even now, I was speaking almost daily with my contact there, working out the final details of what was to be a six-week sabbatical from Boeing devoted to my very first mission outreach. I was to be "sent out" by Frontier to Turkey where I was to conduct, in effect, a "marketing study" of the entire Turkish Church, laying out in some detail the location, membership, and specific orientation of each part of this unique body. The study resulting from my efforts was to be used by Frontier as a basis for them to determine how to proceed with evangelistic outreach to that very large and diverse land. Needless to say, as a missions major at Faith Seminary, I was both thrilled and delighted by this wonderful prospect that seemed to fit so  well into my background and orientation. I had already traveled extensively in Turkey during my Air Force years, and now I was doing so with Boeing, so I felt both prepared and challenged. I could hardly wait for the upcoming summer and the beginning of this new adventure.

"The Lord has shown me something very special and challenging in your immediate future, Bob," Daniel pronounced one morning over coffee. "You are going to be called to an opportunity in some Middle Eastern country. I'm not sure which, but the Lord will be watching very carefully as you either choose to accept or reject this challenge."

"So, what's new, Daniel?" I responded knowingly. "I'm well aware of all this, and so are you! This must be a confirmation of my mission trip to Turkey—your vision fits right in with this."

"Perhaps," he replied, somewhat indulgently. "But, just maybe, the Lord has something else entirely different than Turkey in mind, something more permanent."

There I was, once more, totally discounting Daniel's input. "Just what may that be?" I asked sarcastically.

"I guess we'll have to wait and see," he said.

About two weeks later, I was talking on the phone with my contact at Frontier, further developing the details of my upcoming outreach to Turkey. We finished our conversation, and as I hung up, quite satisfied with how our planning was progressing, suddenly, and even frighteningly,  I  found myself physically unable to remove my hand from the instrument I had just returned to its cradle. Something compelling—it was that still quiet voice telling me, clearly commanding me: "Call them back!" I obeyed, not having a clue why I was calling or what I was to say as I re-dialed the number.

My contact answered and the Lord, to my wonder, gave me the words; utterly strange, unthinkable words, entirely foreign to my own understanding. It was if I were an outside observer rather than a participant in this conversation. "Do you have any contacts in Israel?" I asked matter-of-factly.

My friend at Frontier was also perplexed. "Why in the world are you asking this, Bob?" he replied, obviously puzzled.

"I really don't know myself," I answered forthrightly. "I just *need* to know, do you have any contacts in Israel?"

"Well," he hesitated for a moment, then decided to answer my forthrightness in kind. "We do have one name listed, someone named Kenneth Crowell."

"What do you know about this Kenneth Crowell?" I interrupted.

"Only that he is affiliated with something called the 'Gal Group' in Tiberias, nothing more."

"Is this 'Gal Group' connected with the Church?" I asked, hoping for more information.

"Sorry," my friend replied, "but that's all the information I have. I do have his address if you want it," he added.

"By all means," I replied, then wrote down how I might contact this stranger for reasons unknown to me at the time.

I simply *knew* I must write to this Kenneth Crowell, and I spent that entire evening composing a letter. I told this Mr. Crowell, whoever he was, all about my being Jewish, about my Christian walk, my Air Force career, and my current job as Boeing marketer. I told him about my upcoming trip to Turkey and about my future call to missions as I understood it at the time.

Finally, I confessed that I had no idea *why* I was writing him, a total stranger, not even knowing for certain that he was a believer, only that I was doing so in obedience.

As the weeks turned to months with no forthcoming response to my letter, I put this seemingly bizarre matter out of my mind as having been just one of those "strange" misunderstandings along the way. It really didn't matter to me since by now, even Daniel, my ever-searching, ever-questioning dearest friend, was beginning to share my excitement as the planning for my outreach to Turkey continued to gel.

Thus I wasn't at all prepared for the phone call I received at home one evening in late February.

"Bob Fischer?" the voice at the other end of the line had replied questioningly to my "Hello."

"Yes, this is he," I replied *proforma*, immediately sensing in my spirit that this was an important caller.

"This is Ken Crowell. Sorry to be so long in getting back to you. I'm in Chicago and thought it was high time I answered your letter."

"Mr. Crowell," I replied, my mind racing, trying to attach some sense of reality to the flood of possibilities that were racing through my mind. "It is so good to hear from you."

"Please, Bob," he said, getting right to the point as if he were someone with a very specific agenda. "Tell me more about your marketing experience."

"The fact is," I replied, immediately trying to change the focus, "I pretty much gave you an overview of my experience in my letter. My *real* interest," I continued earnestly, trying to sound convincing, "is mission outreach. I'll be wrapping up my seminary training next summer, and I'm hoping for a call from the Lord in this new direction."

"Tell me more about your *marketing* experience," Ken repeated, unable to conceal from his voice just a hint of his amused understanding. "Specifically, what have you been doing for Boeing?"

What can it hurt, I thought as I began to recount an overview of my international marketing activities of the past almost nine years, while my intent listener occasionally interrupted to clarify a point. "I guess that's about it," I finally concluded.

"Bob, I'll be at the Baptist Retreat Center near Santa Fe, New Mexico, this weekend. Any chance you can fly down on Saturday and spend the evening and part of Sunday with me? I'd love to meet you in person and spend some time with you. I think I may have something of interest for you."

I didn't hesitate for even a moment. The Holy Spirit had already filled me with almost uncontrollable excitement. I *heard* myself responding, "Yes, by all means, I'll plan on coming. Should I rent a car and meet you at the center?"

"No," he responded warmly. "I'll meet you at the small airport there. Just give me a call to let me know what time you'll be arriving."

I arrived in Santa Fe late Saturday afternoon. I became delightfully aware that there was already a hint of spring in the air as I emerged from the small commuter jet and began to take in the beautiful landscape. A few wildflowers were already blooming in just-turning-green meadows at the foot of still snow-covered peaks that surrounded the place. I could feel the very presence of the Creator Himself and I had to struggle to re-focus on the purpose of my visit.

As I walked across the tarmac, it became obvious that the three men waiting there at the out of doors gate were waiting for me. There was an immediate recognition from both sides. "Ken Crowell?" I inquired, beginning to extend my hand to the nearest of the three.

"No, Bob," the white-haired, obviously warm and gracious gentleman with sky blue, 'Holy Spirit-filled' eyes replied glowingly while shaking my hand. "I'm Harold Kent. This is Ken," he continued, introducing me to the second nearest of the three.

"Thanks for coming, Bob," Ken greeted me as we shook hands and he gave me a non-intimidating, quick once-over that was, to my experienced eyes, the obvious   beginning of an extensive three-person interview.

I immediately liked the man and felt entirely comfortable in his presence. His thick covering of brown hair, just turning gray, framed a square-shaped face, complementing his somewhat stocky build. All in all, he projected a blend of strength, self confidence, and determination. My immediate assessment, which later proved to be "spot on," was that here, before me, stood the epitome of a  conservative, fundamentalist Christian.

"Meet Gary Nelson," Ken introduced the third of my greeters. "You two have a lot in common. Gary is a retired Air Force Colonel."

"I'm delighted to meet you, Gary," I said with genuine sincerity as we shook hands, sensing that I had in him a "friend in the camp."

Ken wasted no time getting on to the matter at hand as we began walking toward the nearby  lot where they had parked their rented van.

"Harold and Gary work with Galcom, one of my companies," he explained. "Harold and others fund many thousands of low-cost, fixed-tuned radio receivers that we produce in Israel. Then Gary, who runs our American office in Tampa, distributes them to the mission field.

I was immediately hooked and remained riveted to Ken's continuing orientation to the Gal Group and its several subordinate companies in Israel as we drove the half-hour journey from the airport to  the Baptist Retreat Center.

Ken's wife, Margie, joined us for dinner where the conversation turned to Israel, their adopted country where they had served the Lord for the past seventeen years. Israel was a subject I knew nothing or precious little about, so I asked many questions, all the while trying to absorb the huge amount of new information that unceasingly poured out from my hosts.

Central to what they provided about Tiberias was their own testimony. I found it fascinating that they had long ago been called as "tent makers" and in response, had established their core company, Galtronics, which now had evolved into the world's leading producer of antennas for mobile and cell phones, a new market that was just coming into its own. Ken was especially excited that this company was about to pass the ten million dollar sales threshold, thrusting it into what many would consider a world-class operation.

"The problem," Ken explained, "is that we have grown *too* fast, and we are woefully inexperienced and ill-equipped to expand into large scale international operations. We are essentially a Church-oriented organization, and a large portion of our staff are primarily Church people, not professionally trained and properly experienced technical or business specialists."

I was both fascinated and challenged. "What is your sales and marketing organization and approach?" I ventured.

"We'll talk a lot more about this later," Ken replied. "But first, Margie and I would like to tell you more about Israel in general and about Tiberias in particular before she leaves us alone to discuss business."

Later, Harold and Gary provided a perfect complement to Ken as they together laid out a detailed and deeply interesting description of Ken's unique concept of "tent making." He had founded his company with the intention to initially staff it primarily with Church- oriented people from abroad and then to gradually take on new employees drawn from the local economy.

Over the course of the evening, Harold and Gary made it clear that Ken had been very successful in drawing local people into the company, some of whom had already become believers. Along with encouraging the development of this small but steadily growing, new, indigenous body of believers, Ken was warmly accepted and often praised by the local community as both a upstanding member and a generous employer.

Ken yawned, then paused to look at his watch, interrupting what had been an intense and continuous exchange for the past several hours since Margie had made her promised exit. "Well, gentlemen," he sighed, obviously exhausted from the long effort, "it's nearly one o'clock and it's time we got to the bottom line. Galtronics needs an experienced Director of Sales and Marketing, and from all I can tell, Bob, you are perfectly equipped for the job."

Now was the time, I felt, to be perfectly honest. "In some ways, Ken, I *am* qualified for the job you've outlined, but in other ways I am not."

"Like what?" Ken interrupted, trying to intercept what he sensed was a forthcoming rejection.

"My nearly nine years with Boeing have been focused on developing and selling multi-billion dollar electronic systems. I'm the guy up front who presents top level concepts to the customer hierarchy. When it comes to all the supporting sales and marketing disciplines like product development, public relations, advertising, and all the rest, I have large expert staffs at my disposal to plug in just what I need when I need it. From what I understand, none of this expertise is available in your company."

Ken responded without hesitation. "Bob, you understand *all* the concepts. Surely it would not be a big deal for you to scale down your billion-dollar approach to our million-dollar requirement. What you don't know right now, you can learn from experience as you go along."

I paused for just a moment, then went right to the point. "I take it, Ken, you are seriously considering me for this position? I wish I was a bit more certain at this point what the Lord has in mind?"

"*Exactly!*" Ken answered. "Let's close in prayer and then individually seek the Lord about all this. I'm sure His will in this will be much clearer after we've had some sleep."


I did indeed seek to understand the Lord's will in the privacy of my room, and as I did so, quite predictably, satan and his legion of demons had another plan. I was bombarded with an attack of self-doubt and discouragement. The negatives came in a flood. How could I even *think* about leaving Boeing when I was only two years away from a second pension even larger than the one I was already receiving from the Air Force? How could we even think about giving up this life we had come to love: a more than generous income, first class international travel, prestige—How could I even *dream* of imposing something like this on Donna? How could I take her away from our children and grandchildren after all the sacrifices she had already made as an Air Force wife for nearly thirty years? "O, Lord," I cried out, "surely, this isn't what you have for me?"

Then, it was satan, not God, that responded. I was filled with an overwhelming sense of inadequacy. A specific list of my professional shortcomings appeared accusingly and clearly before my inner eye, like a surrealistic parade of movie credits from which I could not escape repeated notice. What did I know about tapping into already available technical marketing research; how to operate within a tiny marketing budget; how to exploit the day to day lower level mini-media outlets; the specifics of establishing an effective advertising program.... The list went on and on.

I was on my knees by the side of the bed. "O, Lord!" I cried out again. "In the name of Yeshua, please show me what I am to do. O Lord God of Israel, please, give me peace!"

Suddenly, I was overcome with a total sense of relief. I was extremely tired; I looked at my watch. It was nearly three o'clock. I fell into bed and was immediately deep in a totally undisturbed sleep. When I awoke, only three hours later, I felt totally rested and at complete peace. The Lord had answered. While I had no idea what was to follow or how He would implement the plan He had for me, I knew with perfect assurance that I was to trust and obey Him and continue to seek His will. I no longer had the slightest doubt that He would lead me step by step along the pathway He had so carefully laid out for me even before He had formed the earth.

I showered, packed, and got dressed, then hurried to join my hosts for breakfast. I didn't for a moment entertain even the slightest notion that each of them had reached the same conclusion about what the Lord had ordained for my immediate future. All of this became abundantly clear to me as our discussion over breakfast continued on until early afternoon, and it became apparent that we had to hurry to the airport in order for me to catch my late afternoon flight back to Seattle.

It was Margie who first broached a new subject as we drove towards the airport. "Bob, you *are* totally Jewish, isn't that right?"

"Yes, I am," I replied, "on both sides."

"The important thing is," Margie went on, "can you *prove* it? You need to have documentary evidence in order to make *aliyah*."

I had no idea what she meant. "What is *aliyah*?"

Ken answered. "As a Jew, you can emigrate to Israel. This is called *aliyah*. There are many advantages in doing this. You don't have to worry about work visas, and you get some really significant financial assistance from the government to help you resettle in your new country."

It took me a few moments to catch my breath and collect my thoughts. "Pardon me," I finally exclaimed, "but all this sounds rather final. Emigrating would mean giving up my American citizenship, and this is, to say the least, a pretty monumental step—"

Ken laughed. "Oh, no," he replied reassuringly, "there is an arrangement between the two countries that would allow you and your wife to be dual citizens. You wouldn't have to give up *anything*," he chuckled at his own humor before continuing. "Nothing, except, of course, your entire way of life."

Margie got back into the conversation. "Bob, it is very important that you gather all the documentation you can find proving you are Jewish, especially on your mother's side."

"That might be quite a challenge," I replied, feeling a first twinge of concern. "Our family has kept being Jewish a big secret for two generations. What kind of documentation will I need?"

"Being a gentile, I'm by no means an expert on this," Margie answered, "but from what I understand, a letter from a rabbi, a wedding certificate, birth and death certificates, and other solid things like that are what will be needed."

Ken added, "In fact, as I understand it, the usual requirement is for *two* separate documents proving that your mother was Jewish."

I had a tight feeling in my stomach. "That *will* be a challenge that only the Lord can meet," I replied. "But for some reason, I just know all of this is going to be provided."

With that, we had reached the airport, and as Ken drove up to the departure area he turned to another subject. "Bob, there are a couple of things we haven't discussed. The first is salary," he said somewhat apologetically. "I can't begin to match Boeing—

you know, we are a small, mission-oriented company."

"I wouldn't expect you to," I replied as I exited the van and proceeded to retrieve my carryon. I found myself joyfully willing to accept something even as little as half of my current salary. Really, all I needed was enough to live on comfortably. "I'll be looking forward to receiving your formal offer," I relied confidently. "I'm sure it will be perfectly satisfactory."

"The other thing," Ken added in conclusion, "I'd like to invite you to attend our annual sales meeting in Tiberias on May 17. If you can make it, the trip is on us, and it will give you a chance to look us over a bit and to meet our people. Since you've never been to Israel, it only seems fair that you at least have a look before you commit to becoming a citizen."

"I gratefully accept," I replied, as we waved warmly to one another and they drove away.

While I felt a twinge of sympathy for the airline, I was more than a little grateful for the light passenger load on this particular flight, and especially so for the empty row of three seats where I was sitting. As it was my natural and well practiced propensity to sleep on airplanes, I very much looked forward to some badly needed rest on the long trip home. The incredible, life changing events of the past day flooded into my head as I stretched out and closed my eyes. Once again, I could feel a resurgence of the enemy's attack as a flood of doubts became intermingled with and started once again to dominate my thinking. How would Donna react to all this? How quickly could we sell our house and do all of the other things that needed to be done for such a major relocation? How in the world was I going to find any documentary evidence that I was Jewish, a fact I had been trying to suppress for most of my life to this point? Then, once again, just as I fell asleep, the shopping list of my supposed professional shortcomings became manifest in my thinking, passing in turn in a threatening review, giving rise to yet another wave of self-doubt. "O, Lord, I whispered," as I drifted off. " In the name of Yeshua, help, me."

I awoke to the pilot's announcement that we were beginning our descent into Seattle-Tacoma Airport and that we would be landing in about twenty minutes. I awoke slowly from a very sound sleep with the usual sense of unreality, trying to get my bearings in this unfamiliar place. I became aware that I was still stretched out along the full length of the three seats, my head towards the aisle. The cabin of the nearly empty flight had been darkened to accommodate those like me who had chosen the escape of sleep. I found myself looking across the aisle at the row immediately in front of my own. I tried to apply some sense of reality to the image my eyes was attempting to transfer to my brain as a genuine perception, but I had trouble doing so. Perhaps I was still asleep, and this was a dream, I challenged myself. I deliberately blinked my eyes open and shut a few times to test this unspoken theory, but no, I wasn't asleep and what I was seeing wasn't a dream, but rather a reality.

She was quite beautiful, this young woman, perhaps in her mid-twenties, who was beckoning to me with a profound out-pouring of love that covered me entirely, like an imaginary, yet somehow real down-filled comforter, and penetrated to the very depths of my being. She had very large, dark brown eyes that stood out prominently against her picture perfect, porcelain-like, olive-colored Middle Eastern complexion. Her unique counte-nance was made all the more lovely by what appeared to be a supernatural illumination, the source of which was not apparent, giving a strange, heavenly glow to her entire presence.

Once again, I blinked my eyes to test the reality of the moment, and once again, I knew what I beheld was, in fact, real. I tried to focus on the cover of the open book that she held in her two hands and was extending across the aisle to me, as if it were an offering. I read the title, *Guerrilla Marketing,* trying to take in its meaning; then, the sub-title, "Secrets for Making Big Profits From Your Small Business," and the author, Jay Conrad Levinson.

She must have known my strange blend of confusion and awe as she spoke simply, "This is for *you.*"

Just then, at that very moment, as I struggled to frame a response, the cabin of the aircraft was once again fully illuminated as the flight attendant announced our imminent landing. I immediately noted that my visitor from across the aisle had returned to her sitting position, and so did I. However, as I fastened my seat belt, I resolved that I would certainly confront this lovely creature as soon as we had landed to confirm what I had already come to understand was a miraculous happening.

"Pardon me." I approached the young woman the moment she had risen from her seat and turned in my direction. "What was the book you were holding in my direction?"

"Oh, yes," she replied warmly. "It is *Guerrilla Marketing.* It has to do with the challenges of converting the sales and marketing skills needed by a large corporation to those of a relatively smaller one. It is for *you.*"

With that, she smiled, made her way past me as I stood there, for the moment speechless, and headed towards the exit.

It was, by now, quite late on a Sunday evening, a time when Seattle-Tacoma Airport is largely deserted. There were many shops in the airport, but I knew of only one bookstore, Benjamin Books. Noting that all of the many other shops were already closed, I nevertheless hurried toward this one bookstore which I knew to sell mostly paperback novels and periodicals. Surely, I challenged myself testing my own sanity, even if this bookstore was by some wild chance still open, why in the world would I think that they would have such an obscure offering as the book I was now urgently seeking to purchase?

To my absolute amazement, while there was not another soul

in sight in this distant satellite extension of the airport, Benjamin Books was *open*. I rushed in, trying not to convey my excitement to the solitary attendant. I *knew* that the miracle of my encounter with an angel on the airplane was continuing. I therefore wasn't surprised to find there, inexplicably placed among the many pulp novels, one copy of *Guerrilla Marketing*. As I joyfully paid for the book, it occurred to me that it had been written by a Jewish author and offered by a Jewish owned and operated book store. I almost ran to the nearest place where I could sit down.

With trembling hands and filled with anticipation I excitedly opened the book turning first to the Table of Contents. There, before my eyes, in the same order and expressed in the same manner, was the list of specific concerns I had first seen in my mind's eye in Santa Fe, and then again later, just before I fell asleep on the flight home. Praise be to the Lord God of Israel! He had indeed sent an angel before me to keep me in the way and to bring me into the place which He had prepared.

As usual, even after our short times apart, I was filled with a sudden rush of joy and love as I saw Donna waiting for me by the baggage claim area. Our eyes met, as we waved to one another excitedly.

"How was your trip?" she asked, hardly able to contain herself after our welcome home embrace.

"Wow!" I exclaimed, "Have I got a story to tell you—I hardly know where to begin! Let's go home, pour a couple glasses of wine and I'll tell you all about one of the most amazing experiences of my life."

"Ohhh, no!" she begged, insistently. "Please tell me *now*, and on the way home! I can't stand not knowing; not for another minute!"

"Okay, you asked for it!" I said teasingly. "For starters, how would you like to relocate to Israel—I mean *permanently*, like in *emigrate*??"

I had a weird sense of *deja vu*—perhaps it was a word of knowledge. In any event, I *knew* precisely  how Donna would react and respond: just exactly the way she had  some *thirty-three* years ago, when, while still on my knees after asking her to be my wife, I had fearfully told her I was  a Jew.

"Oh, *yes*!!" she exclaimed excitedly. "When do we leave? Oh Sweetheart!!! There is so much for us to do—!!!"

## Chapter Five

## *Aliyah*: Preparing the Way for the Journey Home

> *It shall come to pass in that day that the LORD shall set His hand again the second time to recover the remnant of His people who are left, from Assyria and Egypt, from Pathros and Cush, from Elam and Shinar, from Hamath and the islands of the sea. He will set up a banner for the nations, and will assemble the outcasts of Israel, and gather together the dispersed of Judah from the four corners of the earth.* (Isa 11:11-12)

"Hello, Mickey!" I greeted the almost total stranger who, to my bidding, had answered his phone in a faraway Long Island community. "This is your nephew, Bob Fischer, your sister Lillian's son. Do you remember me?"

"Bobby?" he relied tentatively. "How long has it been since we've heard from you - twenty, maybe thirty years?? Why are you calling now, God forbid, has someone died - who??"

"No, Mickey. Nothing like that. I'm calling to ask for your help. You see, my wife Donna and I are going to make *aliyah* to Israel and I need to prove that I'm Jewish in order for us to become citizens."

"You mean you are actually going to move to Israel *permanently*?? Such craziness—It must come from Alfred's side? Never mind. Bobby, *of course* you are Jewish. How else can I help you?"

"Mickey, I need *documentary* evidence, not just your word."

"Like what kind of evidence?"

"Did Grandma Amelia leave you with any documents - like, for example her marriage *ketubah* or any other official thing signed by a rabbi?"

The silence at the other end of the line seemed interminable. Finally, my long lost uncle continued. "Nothing I can think of," he offered, his voice conveying his genuine disappointment, which didn't begin to match my own. "I'm so sorry."

I wasn't about to so easily dismiss this one remaining family connection. "Where are your parents buried?" I ventured.

"How interesting you should ask, Bobby. In fact, I went out to the cemetery just last week for the first time in at least twenty years."

"What cemetery?" I asked, as I felt a surge of renewed hope begin to rise, as I somehow anticipated his reply.

"Mount Carmel, of course! Where else? It's the only big *Jewish* cemetery on Long Island."

My sudden surge of joy left me speechless for a moment and unable to reply, during which time Mickey shared an even more poignant revelation.

"You know it really is amazing how close our family was. Both of my parents and my grandparents from both sides are all buried together there in the same plot. In fact, this impressed me so much that I asked the cemetery manager to document this unusual situation for me in a letter—It just came a couple of days ago."

I was astounded by what I had just heard, still unable to speak. "Bobby?? Are you still there??"

"Mickey, did I hear you right? You have a letter from the manager of a Jewish cemetery documenting that my grandparents and great grandparents on my mother's side are buried there and were therefore, obviously Jewish?"

There was a momentary silence as Mickey considered my proffered complexities of familial relationships. "Yes, that's exactly right," he replied. Then, with sudden recognition, sharing the same amazing conclusion I had already reached, "You know, Bobby, that letter must be for *you.*"

"It's *here!*" Donna greeted me excitedly one early May evening as I arrived home from work, and she rushed to meet me at the door while clutching an official looking envelope.

"What's here?" I asked, after our welcoming kiss.

"Your Grandma Amelia's birth certificate!" she responded with feigned annoyance by my seeming lack of enthusiasm. "This is the last of the birth certificates! It links *you* directly to your Jewish relatives buried on Long Island. Surely, that should be enough proof for anyone."

"Would that it were," I responded knowingly. "I need *two* major proof documents and, so far, all I have is *one* with a bunch of smaller ones that confirm its authenticity. I need something else; something totally different and equally convincing."

"Like what, Sweetheart? What else could there possibly be??"

"As a matter of fact, Sam (my secretary) suggested that I give the Mormons a call since they are so much into genealogy—so I did. They said it was unlikely they could help me directly, but they suggested that I look into the United States census taken in 1920. They said it was just released for public consumption last week, when the required  privacy hold of seventy years had expired."

"How could that possibly help?" Donna replied skeptically.

"It may be a long shot, but for the first and last time this particular census asked for the 'place of birth' and 'mother tongue' of both the respondent's and his parents. Just maybe, if I can find what certain of my key relatives had to say, it just might provide *some* kind of help."

Donna shared my  skepticism. "Boy, that really does sound like a long shot—but isn't this whole thing almost impossible anyway. Surely, you don't plan to go to Washington D.C. to research this in the national archives?"

"That's one of the compelling things about all this, as vague as it may seem," I replied with measured excitement. "This just released census data is available to the public in several regional offices of the National Archives—one of these just *happens* to be here in Seattle. Guess where I'm going to spend the day tomorrow?"

The normally horrendous, Seattle morning rush-hour traffic had been seriously compounded by an unrelenting torrential downpour replacing, for a time, the usually persistent drizzle, adding its own torment to the nearly two-hour, creeping transit from the extreme south of the city, where we lived, to the extreme north and the Seattle Regional Office of the National Archives and Records Administration.

I tried to pray away the extreme oppression I felt as I pulled into the large and already-crowded parking lot of this dressed-up warehouse-like facility. I noticed that  my hands were unexplainably shaking as I shut down my car, reached for my umbrella, and made a beeline through the downpour toward the front entrance. As I stepped inside this huge, totally unfamiliar, and strangely foreboding  place I had an almost irresistible desire to turn and run as fast and as far as I could carry myself away from this place. Then, in a sudden flash of recognition, I understood the source of this inexplicable negative wave that nearly overcame me to the point where I was beginning to feel dizzy and nauseated. Satan and his legion of demons were not much pleased with  what I was doing and they were trying with all in their power to prevent me from continuing. I took a deep breath, then proceeded to the information desk where I stood in a long line for about thirty minutes before it was my turn to be served. It was worth the wait. The volunteer who greeted me, a middle-aged woman with a captivatingly warm smile, immediately restored my sense of peace and purpose. She seemed genuinely fascinated with my quest for  documentation of my Jewish heritage, and she made every effort to give me a detailed road map on how I might explore the mountains of data stored on microfiche within this facility. By the time she had finished her lengthy orientation, and I had taken extensive notes to memorialize her guidance, I had once again grown quite excited about this adventure, and was even beginning  to feel somewhat optimistic that it might eventually bear some meaningful fruit.

"The key to success," my newly found mentor explained, " is knowing the correct name, spelling, and specific address of the relatives you are seeking on the very day they were interviewed by a census taker in early January 1920. You can be sure that this record is preserved on  film someplace in this facility. The trick is to find it."

The hours had flown by. I looked at my watch noting that that there was only another fifteen minutes before the facility  closed at four-fifteen. My head was spinning from lack of food and what had been an uninterrupted several-hour search. I stared at the microfiche reader before me and noted once again that the census taker's form before me bore no name of any person that looked in any way connected to me,  much less in any way that might indicate that any of them were or were not Jewish. I had looked at literally hundreds of such records throughout the long day, all to no avail. Legions of Fischers, Gelsons, Silvermans and Meyers had paraded before my eyes, and not a single one of them was in any way seemingly connected to me. I was more than deeply disappointed when I closed this last of my already several-times-reviewed film records and shut off the monitor. I felt devastated, even spiritually abandoned.

The drive home through the "flip side" of this morning's congestion was even worse than my earlier experience. If anything, the rain had increased and the visibility had been reduced to literally nothing. Inevitably, I found myself caught in several long and seemingly endless traffic jams.  Finally, after more than three hours, I stormed through the door of our house, slammed it behind me, and headed for the quiet of our den. Donna quietly followed along behind me. Wisely, she had learned over our many years together to remain silent when I was caught up in what  was, hopefully, my rare, roaring-like-a lion state of mind.

"As bad as all that?" she finally ventured tentatively, after we had sat silently together for a few minutes.

"Worse!" I sighed. "It was a total waste of time. I've got a mammoth headache, and I'm *never* going to go near that awful place again! I've never been under such a spiritual attack—in fact, I never have known what it really meant to be under attack before this miserable experience!"

I had begun to recover some sense of peace when I greeted my secretary, Sam the next morning as I walked by her desk outside of my office.

"How did it go at the archives yesterday?" she asked with genuine interest, apparently fascinated by this unusual pursuit of her boss.

"Let me put it this way Sam," I replied, echoing my earlier pronouncement to Donna. "There is absolutely *no way* I am ever going  back there!"

With that, I sat down at my desk and sighed as I took in the mound of paperwork that had collected for my attention during the fruitless day I had been away. Then, as I paused for a moment of prayer before proceeding with the various tasks at hand, a very recognizable "still quiet voice" spoke from within my being. "Go back, my son. Go back *right now!*"

"O, Lord!" I replied in a low and exasperated whisper. "Surely, if it is you who are speaking to me, you must be kidding?"

"Go back, my son," the voice inside me repeated. "Go back *right now!*"

This second journey north was far less tedious than the one the day before. The morning traffic had pretty much abated because of my later start, and the torrential downpour  had diminished to the usually persistent drizzle that characterized our nearly year-round local climate. None of this, however, made me any more certain about what was to follow as I once again pulled into the now familiar, nearly full parking lot, exited my car, and walked towards the entrance to the huge document repository.

"Okay, Lord," I ventured. "It was you, and you alone, who caused me to come back to this place yet a second time, and I don't have a clue what you would have me do. Please, Lord,  in the name of Yeshua, show me."

I must confess, it is a rare thing indeed for me to have such an awesome two-way conversation with my creator, but this was clearly one of those times.

"Go back to the Bronx directory containing the name Gelson," He replied. "Go to the page where Morris Gelson is listed. You will find what you are seeking there."

I recalled with certainty that I had already been over this

ground at least several times the day before, but I was not about
to argue with the King of the universe who had just so clearly told
me that I was to do so yet again. I went straight to the place
where the directories were stored and immediately found the one
He had noted. I was on a roll, and the roll literally continued—in
this case a specific roll of microfiche film, one that had apparently somehow evaded me the day before.

Despite the capacity crowd of researchers in the place, a
microfiche reader became immediately available as I approached
the reading area anticipating a lengthy wait. Within less than five
minutes from the time I entered the building, there before my
eyes was one of the most remarkable sights I have ever beheld.
*Jesus Christ is the same yesterday, today, and forever.*(Heb 13:8)
On January 8, 1920, when one Emma Ackerman, a census taker,
knocked on Grandma Amelia's door, only my Lord Yeshua knew
I would be needing some very special information some seventy-
two years later, that only my Grandma Amelia could provide at
this seemingly unconnected moment in January 1920.

I could almost hear Emma Ackerman ask, "Mrs. Gelson, what
are the names and ages of your children who are living at home?"

Grandma Amelia, always delighting at being the center of
attention gladly and proudly responded. "My Ruthie is fourteen;
my *Lillie* is nine; my Miriam is six; and my Francis is two."

"And, Mrs. Gelson," Emma Ackerman continued, "What is
your native tongue, and what was the native tongue of each of
your parents?"

As I looked at Grandma Amelia's inexplicable response on the
census form as it was long ago, duly recorded by Emma
Ackerman and now appeared to me through the shower of my
own tears of joy, I was overwhelmed by this profound provision
from the Lord. In each of the several blanks calling for "native
tongue" on the page before me, taking in *all* members on both
sides of my mother's family, Emma Ackerman had recorded in

multiple entries the single word "*Jewish.*"  Here before me was the inarguable miracle of my second "proof."

Lillian, my mother, then age nine, was documented as being Jewish on an official Government record, and I, in turn, could easily be tied to this same document as her son,  the son of a Jewish mother.

# Chapter Six

## The Coin of His Realm

*Then Gideon said to God, "Do not be angry with me, but let me speak just once more: Let me test, I pray, just once more with the fleece....(Judges 6:39)*

Donna could hardly contain herself as she rushed to greet me at the baggage carousel. "How was Israel??" she demanded lovingly as we walked toward where she had parked. "Tell me *everything!*" she implored. "Am I going to like our new country?"

I had just returned from a three-day visit to Tiberias as the guest of my soon to be new employer.

"Wonderful!" I exclaimed excitedly. "It was an incredible three days. I hardly know where to begin."

"Tell me *everything!*" she again insisted. "What about Israel??? Tiberias??? Ohhh!!! I'm so excited I can hardly stand it!!"

Both of us were too wound up to sleep, so we talked long into the night, planning, dreaming, repeatedly going over every detail of my three-day experience, all of it blissfully positive. Finally, when we had finished, I reached into my pocket and retrieved a

special gift for my "Ruth" who had married into the covenant of
my people. Lovingly, caught up in a surge of my deep devotion
and great  love for this very special woman whom the Lord had
given me for a life's partner, I presented her with the exquisite  14
kt. gold  Star of David I had purchased in a Sea of Galilee waterfront jewelry shop in Tiberias. We both wept in our shared joy as
she, thrilled by all of this, put this lovely symbol of our new life,
in our soon-to-be new country, on a gold chain and fastened it
around her neck. She has worn it constantly these past, incredible nine years.


    Jack Fiscus, the general manager of the Boeing division where
I was employed,  greeted me with a broad smile as I entered his
office and took the proffered  chair in front of his mammoth, senior executive, mahogany desk.
    "Bob, I'm a bit shocked," he began. "I knew about your sem-
inary thing, and I have assumed you would eventually pursue the
ministry *after* you retired from Boeing....Bob, pardon me, but
don't you think this plan to dump everything and move to Israel
is a bit precipitate?"
    My immediate supervisor, Ralph Backes, the director of mar-
keting, had given me a "heads-up" that Jack was going to do his
best to persuade me not to leave the company, so I was well-pre-
pared for this meeting. "Jack, I'm sure you know that I love this
company and I am very mindful of how well you have treated
me, but this is something different. Let me try to make you understand. I know that I have been *called* to this new assignment in
Israel by the Lord."
    "Okay," he interrupted, trying not to make his exasperation
with me too obvious. "Let's say that you *have* been 'called.' My
concern is the *timing*, not the call itself. Bob, if you were to wait
just another *two years* you would be eligible for a full company

retirement, and I don't have to tell you  how very generous that will be."

"I understand and appreciate this fully, Jack. The thing is, this is a call for *now*, not two years from now. It is something I *have* to do! I was hoping I could make you understand."

Jack paused for a few moments of contemplation before he replied. "I would be less than honest, Bob, if I didn't tell you that we will really hate to lose you. You have become a very important contributor to this division and you will be very difficult to replace. But, more than this, my greater concern is for you and Donna. Are you really *certain* you want to do this, and do it *now?*

I didn't hesitate. "Yes, Jack, I am absolutely certain."

"Okay, Bob, then you can go with my blessings, but please, on one condition. I want you to do me a very special personal favor."

"What's that?" I asked, puzzled.

"I would like for you to accept a one-year, unconditional leave of absence. You will remain a non-active employee with a full right of return to your current position any time within one year after your departure."

I was deeply touched and appreciative of this generously offered 'security net.' "I very gratefully accept, Jack, but I don't think I will be exercising this option, as attractive and generous as it may be."

"We'll see," he said as we shook hands, and I left his office.


The weeks since my initial, mid-May visit to Tiberias passed quickly as we hurried to get all of the many necessary things accomplished by August 11, 1992,  the date scheduled on our one-way tickets to the Tel Aviv Ben Gurion Airport. While most things were falling into place, satan would not be so easily appeased, and he seemed to have focused his opposition to our upcoming move upon our house with its huge mortgage. For the past several months, the Seattle high-end housing market had been exploding as investors from southern California had continued to fuel a bidding war, driving prices to new all-time highs. We had relished in this, expecting to make a killing on our lovely home while escaping the great, even oppressive financial burden it represented, a burden that could be carried by my generous Boeing salary, but not by my anticipated much lower salary. What had started as an interesting consideration soon became the subject of a rising panic as, on the very day we officially listed the house the market began to teeter and continued to do so for the next few days; and then it precipitously collapsed. Within a very short time, it seemed as if we would be unable to even give away our house, much less sell it at a profit.

Daniel and I had therefore all the more seriously speculated about the level of my anticipated but yet to be offered new annual salary. In the end, the two of us concluded that I could expect an offer in the range of $30 thousand to $40 thousand. Daniel, however, still felt that it could be even more, since my new employer would probably be inclined to make this seemingly "perfect fit" as attractive as possible.

It was thus, when Sam delivered the fax from Tiberias that contained my anticipated "offer of employment" to me in my office, that I could simply not believe what my eyes barely were able to take in. "Daniel," I whispered as I entered his near by office with this fax in hand. "Please, give me a sanity check. Does this really say what I think it says?"

Daniel read the fax carefully, then chuckled uncontrollably as he read out loud: "Position offered: Director of Sales and Marketing. Starting Annual Salary $18,000."

"That's what I thought it said," I replied, my shock and disappointment having popped my bubble of enthusiasm about my anticipated employment situation. "*Eighteen thousand*??" I repeated incredulously. "I paid more than twice that in taxes last year! The cost of living in Israel is even higher than it is here. How can *anyone* live there on a salary like this?"

"Let's get right to the point, Bob," my friend ventured. "Are you going to accept it, reject it, or make a counter offer?"

"I'm *committed*, Daniel!" I replied, trying to convince us both. Of course, I will accept this salary and trust that the Lord will either arrange to sell our house or find some other way for me to keep up the payments!"

Daniel had a vested interest in the next subject. "What about a car? You know, with taxes, new cars in Israel cost more than double what they do here. If you want to renege on our deal, you can keep the Volvo and ship it for a lot less than it would cost to buy a new one."

Earlier, Donna and I had agreed to sell Daniel and Sheryl her car at low book, and I wasn't about to disappoint our best friends. "No, Daniel, a deal is a deal. We'll just trust the Lord to give us wheels when we get there."

Despite my bravado, things seemed to keep getting worse. Not only did the house not sell—almost no one even came to look at it. The battle was waging ever stronger in the heavenlies and the fallout was piling up quite deeply on all sides of this prospective new immigrant to Israel. Donna and I continued to pray with ever increasing intensity about our seemingly impending financial disaster, and even though I tried to conceal the fact from Donna, Daniel, and most importantly from the author of the whole affair, the Lord God of Israel Himself, my own faith began to waver as August 11th drew ever nearer.

About two weeks from my last day at Boeing, I was eating lunch by myself in the company cafeteria nearest my office. As I ate, taking no pleasure in the process, satan provided a roll call of my many uncertainties and concerns. How could we bear being so far away from our children and grandchildren? How could we meet expenses if we were unable to sell our house?

How would a two luxury car family adjust to being a no car family? How could we  worship away from our beloved Beth Simcha fellowship?

"O Lord," I cried out in a whisper that could be heard only by Him. "If this is from you—if we are truly to go to Israel, please give me an *unmistakable* sign." I could hardly believe what I heard myself next saying. I had never dared to challenge the Lord like this before, yet I continued: "If you have really ordained this move to Israel, then let me find some money before I get back to my office. It doesn't matter how much, Lord, a dollar, a quarter, a nickel, or a dime, even a *penny* will be fine."

I immediately regretted casting this fleece, even before I had completed its uttering. I repented for my lack of trust, but even so, as I stood up from the table and started walking the one hundred or so yards  back to my office I meticulously searched every square inch of the carpeted corridor along the way. "O, Lord, forgive me!" I cried out, wondering what I would do if He *didn't* honor this fleece.

Finally, as I reached Sam's for-the-moment vacant desk, having only gotten a strained neck in return for my just-completed meticulous surveillance, I felt devastated, pondering what to do next. Then, just as I took the final step into my office, I glanced downward  to joyfully behold God's amazing and tolerant reply to my fleece. There, right in the middle of the slightly raised threshold at the entrance of my office was a bright shiny new nickel!

The most amazing aspect of this "wonder" to me was that the Lord apparently chose this device of finding a coin as a continuing private covenant with me, His too-often-questioning son. Since that first wonderful coin I found on the threshold of my office and the great significance it had for me, the Lord has made it a point to supply me with a series of coins, one on every occasion since, when I had a serious question about direction that only He could furnish. To my great and continuing amazement, He has supplied me with such a coin sometimes at my own bidding, but more often, even before I could ask.

Soon after we arrived in Israel, I started to save these coins in a growing stack on a wooden Messianic Star of David that hangs in my office at home. Just now, I counted them. As of today, there are ten.

I was filled with a sense of finality, excitement, and anticipation, flavored with a deep sense of the presence of God as I drove the final fifty or so miles into Phoenix in my treasured BMW that I was about to give to our youngest, Julie, and her husband Jon as a gift.

Everything that could be done had been done, I reflected in review. We had disposed of most of the material things we had collected over the years, closed out our affairs in Seattle, and said goodbye to our friends, and the dear ones at Beth Simcha. And I had bid a fond farewell to my fellow workers at Boeing. Finally, with a mixture of great sadness and overwhelming joy, I had locked the door of our still unsold house and pulled out of the driveway for the last time.

Now we had a few days left to spend with the kids in Phoenix before we moved on to our new world. But, at least for a time, the battle had ceased and I was almost overcome with a profound sense of everything good. Donna had flown ahead to Phoenix since we couldn't get both of us and all our luggage into the BMW.

And so, here I was, all alone with my wonderful Lord. I began to sing out to Him, quietly at first, then I grew progressively louder as I beheld the work of His hands in the star-filled Arizona night sky. The wind rushing through the open sunroof and windows provided an initial accompaniment as I sang:

"Halleluia, hallelulia; Hallelulia, hallelulia!"
"Halleluia, hallelulia; Hallelulia, hallelulia!"
Here I was, a *Jew,* one of a very few Jews who knew and loved the Jewish Messiah, Yeshua. Here I was, driving toward a new destiny in Israel.

"Halleluia, hallelulia; Hallelulia, hallelulia!"
"Halleluia, hallelulia; Hallelulia, hallelulia!"

Again and again, I sang out the one beautiful word of this magnificent praise song. How sweet and good! What a joy it was knowing *who* and *what* I was, knowing that I was right in the center of His will. Louder and louder I sang with all of my strength, with all of my soul from the depths of my spirit.

"Halleluia, hallelulia; Hallelulia, hallelulia!"
"Halleluia, hallelulia; Hallelulia, hallelulia!"

How filled with His wonderful presence was this special moment, there in the wilds of the Sonora Desert where the only witnesses were a sentinel army of saguaro cacti in silhouette rushing by on both sides.

And then, suddenly, out of the very halls of heaven, *they* joined me in my singing praises to our beloved Lord. *They* were a huge chorus, perhaps even thousands of angels, singing along with me in what had to be at least sixteen part harmony. It was glorious! Wonderful! I was experiencing an indescribable ecstasy of worship the likes of which I had never before known or even imagined!

"Halleluia, hallelulia; Hallelulia, hallelulia!"
"Halleluia, hallelulia; Hallelulia, hallelulia!"

On and on it continued for at least another twenty minutes, and then, as I began to enter the city, just as suddenly as they had appeared, my heavenly companions were gone. However, I was anything but alone. I was alive in the Spirit and thrilled with anticipation for what lay ahead.

## Part Three

## Thorns Among the Cherries: Taking Up Our Everlasting Inheritance

*On that day I swore to them that I would bring them out of Egypt into a land I had searched out for them, a land flowing with milk and honey, the most beautiful of all lands.* (Ezek 20:6)

## Introduction

*If you want to make a small fortune in Israel, bring a big one.* (contemporary saying)

"Let me tell you, Donna," I almost shouted in my rising frustration, "we are getting into a very serious situation. Can you believe it; not *one single* offer on our house and we've been in Israel for almost a year!"

"Maybe you should calm down and we should thank God together for our many blessings," she quietly suggested.

I wasn't to be so easily and immediately pacified. "It isn't *easy* to remain calm in the face of such adversity—Vanished savings! A continuing huge debt we can't begin to service out of our current income! Not to mention the fact that I'm tired of walking up and down these hills every day, and there's no money in sight for a car!"

"Are you finished??" Donna asked softly as I completed my outburst.

"I suppose so," I relented. "But I never thought our *aliyah* would end up in a crash course on how to deal with spiritual warfare. It's really amazing how satan keeps trying to take away the great joy and blessings of our Israeli citizenship."

Donna sighed, then wisely suggested, "Let's *pray!*"


A few mornings later, I was quietly seeking God's presence as I walked from the bus stop to my office. It was a glorious new day. The late season poppies were laid out in a magnificent red carpet that seemingly decorated every available square inch of otherwise undeveloped space. The view of the Sea of Galilee with the Golan Heights as a backdrop was breathtaking from this top-of-the-hill vantage point, and I stopped for a moment to better take it all in.

"O Lord!" I had the audacity to boldly complain. "It's been almost a year now, and we *still* haven't sold the house. Not a *single* offer! *Why,* Lord? Am I doing something wrong—something against your will?"

Deep within my heart I already *knew* the answer. I had long been struggling with a reality I hadn't wanted to admit, even to myself.

The Lord who called me home to Israel, in a way had set me up. He knew my every weakness, my love for the things of this world made possible by my earlier prosperity. He also knew that my faith alone was not sufficient to enable me to boldly give up all of this and unquestioningly, simply climb on the next flight to Tel Aviv.  He therefore created an  alternative, an alternative appealing enough for me to drop everything and respond.

The offer of the position of "Director of Sales and Marketing" was exactly the divinely ordained carrot I needed. It wasn't a question of salary—I *knew* He would provide for our every material need.  In His great love and intimate knowledge of me, He knew that I needed a *position* to justify my  turning our lives upside down, and this is what He so graciously provided. However, even before we could begin to get settled into our new life in Israel, He showed me that this new employment, once it had served its purpose and gotten me to the Land, was not to be anything like a long term, rest of my life calling.  Instead, from the first day of my employment,  the seeds of its relatively short-term nature began taking root, and as time passed, my desire to move on to something new grew as I continued to pray for whatever it was that the Lord had next planned for me. While I found myself rebelling at the notion in my rising impatience, nevertheless I had no choice.  I *needed* my current salary to meet our continuing monthly obligations. There was no way I could seriously consider moving on until I shed myself of our house in Seattle and the onerous weight of its accompanying financial drain.

Then, as the reality of my situation once again nagged at my innermost being,  I heard the still quiet voice answer accusingly what I already knew, adding yet another dimension to my  self-condemnation. "You have never really made a *commitment* to your current calling." The staggering truth of His judgment cut deep. "Yes, Lord," I replied like a chastised child. "You are right. I have *tried,* but my heart hasn't  been in it.  I know you have something else for me, and I have been waiting for your new direction."

As I stood there among the blood red carpet of poppies, contemplating my situation,  I thought about the shed blood of my

Messiah, Yeshua, and I began to repent. "O Lord, in the name of Yeshua, I ask you to forgive me for holding back. With all of my heart I promise to apply all of my ability and attention to this company and calling. Yes, Lord, I now make a full and unqualified commitment to this work, and I do so in the name of Yeshua."

A few minutes later, as I entered my office, I was filled with a new cheerfulness. I no sooner had taken my seat and begun to shuffle through the paperwork in my in-basket than the phone rang. It was our real estate agent in Seattle. I hadn't spoken with her in several months.

"I've got some *great* news, Bob!" she reported. "You aren't going to *believe* this, but I've just gotten not one but *two* firm offers on your house. They seem to be competing with one another!"

"*Incredible!*" I cried out in thanksgiving as I hung up the phone. "How sweet and how good you are, O Lord, for such an immediate answer to my prayer."

We immediately accepted the better of the two offers, and the sale closed a month later. Two months later, I got a clear impression that the Lord had graciously released me from this present calling and, by mutual agreement with my employer, I moved on to better seek what the Lord had next for me here in the Land.

Now, nine years later, as I consider the ensuing triumphs and the failures, the joyous moments and the sad, and finally the beginnings of sweet success, I can only affirm that none of this would have been possible if the Lord had not so graciously illuminated the way with His never-ceasing signs, wonders, and miracles. Always, at just the right moment of each successive need, He was there holding out a basket for me—a basket full of cherries among which satan had liberally scattered an array of thorns.

Forgive me, O Lord, for in my eagerness to move forward,

without taking time to properly seek Your will and thus make a proper choice, I far too often have found I have foolishly grasped one of satan's thorns, instead of one of Your intended cherries.

## Chapter One

## Planted in the Land

*"So it shall be, when the LORD your God brings you into the land of which He swore to your fathers, to Abraham, Isaac, and Jacob, to give you large and beautiful cities which you did not build, houses full of all good things, which you did not fill, hewn-out wells which you did not dig, vineyards and olive trees which you did not plant...."* (Deut 6:10-11)

"It seems kind of strange, sitting here in the 'back of the bus,'" Donna commented as she squirmed about, trying to get comfortable in the unfamiliar, relatively small seat in the economy class compartment of the  TWA 747.

I tried to make light of our unaccustomed  low end air travel situation. "Look at it this way," I replied. "The good news is we won't have to make a return flight. We only have one-way tickets."

"This does sound a bit final," she ventured. "What happens if we decide this whole thing was a mistake?"

"Then we buy another set of one-way tickets and prepare to eat crow with a lot of folks, starting with Jack Fiscus," I offered lightly, then continued quite seriously. "But this *isn't* going to happen. The Lord God of Israel has called us home to the Land of our inheritance, and we are going there to take Him up on His many promises."

"I *know*," Donna replied, her eyes misting over like my own.

The ancient Ford *monit* (taxi) that carried us from Ben Gurion International Airport to Tiberias was loaded to its maximum capacity with not only us but also with another lady passenger whom the driver had squeezed in with us and all of our baggage for the three-hour journey. Even so, we had been instantly taken with the beauty of our new country as we drove north along the Mediterranean coast, and then turned East for the cross-country final leg to Tiberias.

"It sure will be wonderful just getting there," Donna whispered, forgetting for a moment that our fellow passenger did not understand a word of English.

"What are you complaining about?" I teased. "It's *only* been just over twenty-four hours since we left Phoenix. But I'm with you. I can hardly wait to take up temporary residence in the company's apartment."

"I sure hope we find our own place soon," Donna replied. "It will be so good to have a sense of permanence again."

"Let's not rush it. We have as long as six weeks in these temporary digs. We can take our time and make sure before we sign any contract for a place of our own."

"Ohhh, Donna exclaimed excitedly as she caught her first sight of Tiberias set along the western shore of the Sea of Galilee with the exquisite Golan Heights as a backdrop on the other side of the water. "It's even more beautiful than I had it pictured,

Sweetheart - can you imagine having an apartment with a view like this??"

The driver seemed to be having difficulty finding our temporary residence as he drove slowly along a street crowded with dismal and disheveled looking two-to-four-story apartment buildings. Finally, he pulled the taxi to a stop alongside a huge, overflowing garbage dumpster directly in front of a particularly shabby-looking building and declared proudly in broken English, "We here—You home!"

"There must be some mistake!" I complained. "Are you *sure* this is the right place??"

"We here, You home!" he repeated insistently.

"It's okay, Sweetheart," I tried to reassure both Donna and myself as we extricated ourselves from amongst the suitcases and exited the vehicle. "Remember, this is only *temporary!*"

In our many years of marriage I have never quite understood how my darling, professionally trained and long-experienced-nurse wife, on one hand, was able to tolerate the most gory of human blood-and-guts situations, while on the other, was totally unable to cope with two of God's creatures: snakes of any variety, and cockroaches of all sizes, shapes and persuasions. It was thus that when it became immediately apparent that our otherwise adequate temporary residence for two was in fact the permanent residence of many cockroaches, that we accelerated our quest of permanent quarters.

I got away with dismissing Donna's first sighting of a large "tree roach" hurriedly making its way across our kitchen floor as an isolated incident. She bought this story until presumably this same creature, together with several other members of its family, reappeared within the next few hours.

"You've got to get me out of here!" Donna insisted when I could find no other way to explain away our co-residents.

"Hang in there, Dear!" I pleaded. "We already have an agent looking for a place, and you can be sure he will find one soon."

"Look at this! Just look at this!!" Donna commanded, directing my attention to a bottle of Vitamin A capsules that she had, just hours before, placed on a small shelf above the kitchen sink.

I immediately complied, noting that the bottom of the plastic bottle had somehow gotten cracked. Even more curiously, I noted that several of the gelatin capsules were lined up in a neat row on the shelf, just beyond the cracked opening.

"Nuuu???" I replied, not understanding what my by-now-quite-agitated wife was trying to show me.

"Just pick up one of those capsules and *look* at it!!" she demanded.

I did so, noting with surprise that the gelatin case of the capsule that should have contained a dark, oily liquid was now, mysteriously, quite empty. Upon closer examination, I could see that a small hole had been bored in one end of the now empty shell. As I confirmed that all of the rest of the "empties" were similarly "bored," the reason for the increased traffic of our "friends" to and from the kitchen area became quite apparent.

"Look at it this way," I tried to make light of the situation. "These fellows may now have the greatest eyesight in the world, but they have surely ruined their livers and don't have long to live."

That my pronouncement was far from the end of the story became clear when Donna returned from her first shopping expedition to a local neighborhood *makolet* (convenience store).

"It took a while to make myself understood," she pronounced, "but I managed to buy *this*," she reported, proudly presenting for my view an aerosol can with dead cockroaches pictured on its Hebrew language label. She then immediately declared war, almost shouting, "I'll show these little monsters that there isn't room for both them and me in this place," as she went through every room in the apartment, spraying wherever she imagined that any such objectionable creature might be lurking just out of sight.

Unfortunately, her frontal attack strategy backfired in a big way. Instead of killing the literally hundreds of roaches with which we shared these quarters, her assault had instead "flushed" them from each of their many hiding places, and within minutes, there were legions of the enemy madly scurrying about virtually every square inch of the apartment.

Somehow, the absurdity of the situation, Donna rushing about attacking the army of invaders with gusto until her ammunition was exhausted, caught my sense of humor, and I began to laugh, then howl, almost out of control. Donna rushed into my arms, and for a few moments, she joined me in my outrageous hilarity. Then, as we sat there, arm in arm on the kitchen floor of the company's apartment, surrounded by a legion of dead and dying cockroaches, we were both suddenly overcome by the utter strangeness of our new situation, and we began to weep together in a potpourri of mixed emotions.

God is great and good in His mercy. Early that same evening, our agent, Ilan, an enterprising, part-time real estate person, called to say he had an apartment he would like to show us that met our stipulated requirements. At this point, given the continuing infestation of our temporary quarters, we were prepared to be not nearly as demanding as we had been when we earlier stated our preference for a penthouse apartment with a view of the lake.

Later that evening, when Ilan escorted us into the elevator of a three-year-old, lovely, five-story building a short distance uphill from the center of the city, we were hardly prepared for the great gift that was about to be unveiled. The two of us immediately shared a sense of intimate belongingness as we stepped from the elevator and were greeted by Amnon and Rachel, the owners of this genuinely lovely dwelling.

We were immediately and totally taken with the place as we surveyed the magnificent salon, very large kitchen and four nice bedrooms, one of which was a delightful master suite. As wonderful as all this was, the crowning glory of the apartment lay in the last thing we were shown, one of the two very large *meerpesets* (balconies), each of which provided a breathtaking, uninterrupted view of the city, the Sea of Galilee and the Golan Heights. After we, had inspected the second equally magnificent *meerpeset* that adjoined both what was to become my home office as well as our guest room, Ilan turned to us and asked simply, "Is this the sort of thing you had in mind?"

Everything was perfect with this the Lord's provision: The location, the layout, the incredible view, even the price. Donna replied for us both. "Never in my wildest imagination did I even consider that such a place might be available."

"We are so happy you are pleased with our apartment," Amnon, said warmly, after we had signed the one-year lease and he, with Rachel by his side, escorted us to the door as we prepared to leave. "Is there anything else we can do for you?"

I had been fascinated by a small olive tree planted in about a one foot high container on the main *meerpeset*. I was especially taken with olive trees since I had reared one in the front yard of our house in Phoenix and had learned how to preserve the fruit with some expertise. "I would really appreciate it if you would leave the olive tree," I replied. "You can be sure I will take very good care of it for you."

"Consider it done," Amnon replied. "It's a very special tree," he explained, "a hybrid that will one day bear many large olives from its branches that have been grafted in to a wild rootstock."

"Thank you so much for entrusting it to our care," I replied, at that point having no way of knowing how *very* special indeed this amazing tree was to become.

## Chapter Two

## The Gospel in a Tree

*For if the first fruit is holy, the lump is also holy; and if the root is holy, so are the branches. And if some of the branches were broken off, and you, being a wild olive tree, were grafted in among them, and with them became a partaker of the root and fatness of the olive tree, do not boast against the branches. But if you do boast, remember that you do not support the root, but the root supports you.* (Rom 11:16-18)

I sighed with the satisfaction of having completed a long effort as I put the final touches on the last of sixty-five overhead transparencies I had prepared over the past several weeks to use during my upcoming *first* speaking tour in the United States. It was a late April evening in 2001, and I was exhausted. I shut down my computer and, as was my custom, I wandered out to sit for a time, and wind down on our main *meerpeset.*

As I paused in front of our very special olive tree, I found it impossible to hold back tears of sadness as I beheld its clearly dying branches.

"O Lord," I pleaded in a whispered prayer, "how could this be? Why would You take this precious tree from us when You have used it with such purpose over these past nine years? In the name of Yeshua, Lord, I ask You to breathe new life into these branches and to make them once more thrive in Your presence and for Your glory."

I felt Donna's comforting presence even before she took her place at my side. "It's dying." I stated the obvious. "I just don't understand it - we've watered it, fed it, prayed over it, yet, nothing seems to work. It just keeps getting worse and worse."

We shared a genuine love for this once-thriving tree and thus found ourselves mourning in a unique sort of *shiva* for our seemingly now- near-dead, special companion. We stood there silently, each lost in our own private recollections as the last glow of a magnificent sunset reflecting in the Sea of Galilee transformed itself into an array of diamond-like stars that were just appearing in the darkening blue-black sky over the Golan Heights. As Donna silently took my hand in her own and squeezed it gently, I somehow sensed we were at that moment sharing the same precious memory:

Once again in the theater of my recollections, it was mid-August, 1992. I found myself strangely depressed at the end of my first workday in Israel, as I exited the public motorbus and began walking the block or so to our temporary quarters, now known to us both as the "Roach Roost."

"How was your day, Sweetheart?" I asked for Donna's report before she could ask for mine, trying to put off for as long as possible the inevitable recounting of my own very confused emotions.

"*Incredible!*" she responded excitedly. "Wait until I tell you what happened!"

"Behold the great white hunter from America!" I teased. "How many more of our little *friends* did you assassinate?"

"As a matter of fact, I've gone through *two* more cans of spray," she reported somewhat proudly, but that isn't the *amazing* thing—something *really* special happened at our new apartment!"

I picked up on her suddenly turned serious mood. She seemed filled with awe as she struggled to find words to describe what had no doubt been a profound experience.

"You *did* go there as planned to check things out," I ventured curiously, attempting to prompt her revelation.

"*Yes,* I did, late in the afternoon, after Amnon and Rachel had cleared all their things out of the place. As promised, they left the two beds, the TV, and a few kitchen items to tide us over until our container gets here."

"So, what's so profound about that?"

She carefully collected her thoughts before continuing. "Okay," she began, "let me start at the beginning. No one was there when I arrived. When I opened the door and stepped inside, there was absolutely *nothing* in the apartment except the few things they promised to leave. The salon looked huge and very empty." She paused again, looking for words.

"Go on," I encouraged. "What happened next?"

"Well," she hesitatingly continued, "as soon as I locked the door behind me, I took a quick tour, carefully inspecting the entire apartment. First, I walked through the back of the place, you know, all the bedrooms, the bath, and your office. Then, I took a close look at the salon and the kitchen. Finally, I walked out onto the main *meerpeset.*"

"Okay!" I interrupted, taking advantage of her brief pause to catch her breath. "What's so remarkable about any of that?"

"The *olive tree!*" she exclaimed. "You know, the one they

promised to leave for you. Well, it wasn't *anyplace* to be seen in the apartment! When I didn't find it on the *meerpeset,* I went back and looked in every room again, thinking they may have put it aside some place. Well, when I didn't find it this second time, I figured they must have changed their minds and taken it with them."

I tried unsuccessfully to mask my disappointment at this news. "No big deal," I replied unconvincingly. "We can always get another olive tree-- but there *was* something *special* about that particular one."

"You didn't let me finish," Donna continued. "After I didn't find the tree during my second time around the place, I went out on the *meerpeset,* just to make sure I hadn't somehow missed it there. I hadn't—but here comes the really *amazing* part! When I finally turned to leave—well, right there in front of the locked door, blocking my exit, was *your* olive tree, just as it was promised!"

"Perhaps it was there all the time and you just missed it when you came in?" I ventured skeptically.

"Sweetheart, you *aren't* listening! I'm telling you that I would have *tripped* over it had it been there when I came in! It was blocking the door so that it could not be opened!

There isn't any question about it. God put it there for you, and He did it for a purpose."

I felt a sudden confirmation in my spirit. "I'm sure He will make that purpose clear in time," I responded filled with awe.


"It really does look bad," Donna reluctantly proclaimed, pulling me back to the sad reality of this moment, nine years after our amazing first encounter with this now near-dead tree.

"It does," I agreed, as if we had been standing by the death bed of a soon to be departed dear one. "I was really counting on another bumper crop of olives this year," I lamented. "I was hoping for at least twice the 183 we processed in 1998."

"They were delicious," Donna recalled fondly. "And almost the size of plums."

Suddenly, I felt prompted in my spirit to more closely examine our presumably terminally ill potted friend. Tentatively, I scratched away a bit of the outer bark from several of the small top branches furthest away from the trunk. In each case, although there wasn't a hint of life in any of the many absolutely dead clusters of already dried leaves, to my utter amazement, there was a healthy green layer just beneath the seemingly dead surface.

Then, there it was again. *"Look just below the graft."* I heard the unmistakable still voice instructing.

I immediately complied, examining the visible, two-inch, lowest section of the trunk where it emerged from the soil.

"Praise the Lord!" I exclaimed. "Look at this, Sweetheart! This tree *isn't* dead! There's still lots of life in the grafted-in branches—and, there are wild shoots, lots of them, just beginning to spring up from the roots!"

"What do you suppose this means?" Donna ventured.

"I'm not quite sure," I replied. "But I know it won't be long until the Lord reveals to us what He has in mind."

Now, as I continue this writing, in early June 2001, nearly two months later after we discovered renewed life in our seemingly dead tree, I have just returned from my first extended speaking tour in the United States. During the past six weeks I was led, during multiple engagements, to teach on several themes related to the Jewish roots of the Christian Church, including the great significance of the tiny remnant of some two-thousand "born again" Jews that constitute the Body of Yeshua in Israel. Standing here, once again, before my remarkable olive tree after a several weeks absence I am deeply moved by the clarity of the Lord's message for the Church He has made implicit in this crystal-clear, living demonstration of His purpose. I now note with great awe how the many shoots that began from the roots just six weeks ago, prior to my departure from Israel, have now sprung up as lovely, healthy, verdant new branches, each already more than a foot long. I note, also, that on every original grafted-in branch where all of the earlier leaves had died, shriveled up and blown away, many crisp, green, new clusters of healthy leaves have already sprouted, capping what is clearly a remarkable, ongoing resurrection of this amazing tree from near death to emerging, new life.

Praise the Lord! In my spirit He has shown me the meaning of all this. It is an amazing part of His provision for both the believing Jewish remnant in Israel and for the world-wide Gentile Christian Church:

**The Early Years**:   Our special olive tree thrived from the moment we took over its care in August 1992. It grew remarkably fast. Thus it needed to be transplanted successively to ever larger containers until we finally placed it in its current, very large, durable plastic tree container.

The first few plum-sized olives appeared on the grafted-in branches in 1994, and the crop increased with each passing year. Then, inexplicably, beginning in 1999, the tree bore no fruit at all, and the signs that it was beginning to die became more and more obvious. *Nothing* seemed to help—neither careful watering, regular feeding, multiple spraying, nor frequent prayer. Could the tree be root bound, I conjectured? *No*, I quickly concluded. It had been removed to a huge, well-drained pot and had not grown nearly enough to pose such a root restriction situation.

The Word teaches us: *To everything there is a season, a time for every purpose under heaven.* (Eccl 3:1). I see a deep spiritual meaning in these early years of our tree.

The grafted-in branches, I believe,  represent the relatively small part of the Gentile Christian Church that acknowledges, fully understands, and is nourished by its Jewish roots. These are my brothers and sisters in Yeshua who faithfully support, through prayer and by other means, the small, ethnically Jewish believing remnant in Israel.

Year by year, the grafted-in branches of our olive tree grew, even thrived, as their  fruit increased with each harvest. Then, suddenly, in 1999,  the thriving ceased along with the harvest, and the tree began to die.

Why? The answer can be found in recent history. In October 1998, Bill Clinton, the then President of the United States, exerted all manner of pressure upon Benjamin Netanyahu, the then Prime Minister of Israel, in effect, *forcing* him to sign the Wye River Agreement which promised, directly against God's Word, that Israel would eventually "return" the entire so-called "West Bank" (Samaria and Judea) to the terrorist Palestinian Authority in order that they might establish a new, independent "State of Palestine."

From that moment forth, the world and even much of the Church, turned ever more against Israel. One United Nations resolution followed another, condemning Israel for the very fact that it was "occupying" Arab land:  the Land which in fact had been given to the Jewish people as an everlasting inheritance by their God.

All  this was accompanied by a well orchestrated, satanically driven resurgence of replacement theology (the notion that the Jewish people, having failed God, have been replaced by Gentile Christians who have now become the "true Jews"). At the same time, Christian Anti-Semitism (a blind hatred and rejection of the Jewish people) surged within the Church along with a corresponding sympathy and seemingly blind, unquestioning, moral and material support of Israel's historic Arab enemies.

Despite the fact that Ehud Barak, who took the premiership from Netanyahu in a landslide victory in May 1999, offered the "Palestinians" 95% of Samaria and Judea, half of Jerusalem, control of the sacred Jewish sites including the Temple Mount, and even financial support for the to-be-recognized "State of Palestine," God hardened the heart of their leader, Yasser Arafat. Inexplicably, he rejected this incredibly generous offer, demanding, instead, *all* of the Land, an end to the State of Israel and ultimately, what was to be the death of all Jews.

Even so, the United States and, virtually all the rest of the world clamored to support the Palestinian cause. Hateful act followed hateful act. The current vitriolic *intifada* broke forth in late 2000.

Simultaneously, and I feel certain it was a divine illustration, our olive tree stopped bearing fruit and began to die. So, also, did that portion of the once supportive Gentile Christian Church that had ever increasingly begun to take up the pro-Palestinian clamor and to turn its back on Israel.

**Our Tree in Mid-2001**: There is, I believe, a tremendous significance in the return of righteous leadership to both the United States and the State of Israel. Equally significant, I believe, is the incredibly rapid growth of the "Return to the Jewish Roots of the Church" movement under the God-anointed leadership of Barbara Richmond, Sid Roth, Robert Sommerville, John Garth, and several others. It is the essence of this movement that the Lord called me to write about in my second book, *The Children of God*, and to teach about in my just-completed speaking tour in the United States and in those that will follow. Legions of Gentile Christians are recognizing that the roots of their faith are planted deeply in the rich spiritual soil of Mount Zion: not in the pagan-laden muck of Rome. Manifest in this new understanding is that the Bible begins in Genesis (not Matthew). There is a new acknowledgment that Yeshua, His apostles, and much of the Church throughout its first several decades of existence were entirely Jewish. Even while rejecting its satanically inspired pagan practices, celebrations and understandings, the Church is more and more embracing the *Torah* for its spiritual guidance and as a rich storehouse of Jewish tradition as a basis for its praise and worship.

Praise be to the Lord God of Israel! Even while the verdant, filled with new life leaves are springing forth on recently, seemingly dead, grafted-in branches, many thick, vibrantly healthy clusters of wild olive shoots are springing up from still very much alive roots.

By all means, I believe that the once again living, newly-leafed branches represent the reemerging, revitalized Gentile Christian Church which is ever increasingly beginning to recognize and return to its Jewish heritage as it abandons the apostasy of Rome.

I also see here another obvious meaning: the thriving wild olive shoots represent new, revitalized, natural Jewish branches springing up from the irrepressible, miraculously surviving natural Jewish roots. As such, they are, in part, a picture of the rapidly growing remnant of Jewish believers in Israel. For example, since 1995 Barbara Richmond has been in contact with the leaders of a group of now more than four- hundred Orthodox Jews in the Old City of Jerusalem who have embraced their Messiah, Yeshua. This sizable and quickly growing group of new believers say, as the Holy Spirit directs, that they will soon announce their faith to the nation of Israel and to a waiting and spiritually starved world.

Another significant message to be seen in our amazing olive tree is that both the grafted-in branches and the thriving new natural branches springing up as wild shoots are nourished by the same wild olive roots. These roots, I believe, clearly symbolize

Judaism, the one true mono theistic religion with Messiah Yeshua as its head.

The Gentile Christian Church, I believe, is emerging and will eventually be the singular completion and living fulfillment of first century Nazarene Judaism. Further, I see in this near dead but now reborn wonder of our Lord's creating hand, a perfect representation of the unity implicit in both Judaism and the Church which is its completion.

My most fervent prayer is that one day soon fruit will again come forth upon the thus revitalized natural and grafted-in branches of our tree, but much more importantly that spiritual fruit will come forth in abundance from all the branches of the Body of Yeshua that it so wonderfully symbolizes.

# Chapter Three

## Reaching Into the Basket
## A Vision or a Dream?

*And it shall come to pass afterward that I will
pour out My Spirit on all flesh; your sons and
your daughters shall prophesy, your old men
shall dream dreams, your young men shall see
visions.* (Joel 2:28)

Had I, from the outset, fully understood the probability for
success of any, however well conceived and financed new business in Israel, I would have entered into the venture of starting
my own companies  with a lot more trepidation, or more likely
would never even have begun. Later, long after I had taken the
plunge into entrepreneurship in the Land,  I was shocked to learn
that more than eighty percent of new Israeli companies fail
before the end of their first year. Moreover, of the remaining
twenty percent, only five percent remain in business at the end of
five years. Currently, in these days of *intifada,* with the national
economy in an externally imposed state of strangulation, the situation has grown even more grave for any potential

entrepreneur.

There are at least two overriding reasons for this incredibly unfriendly business environment. First, governmental regulation is almost unbelievably suffocating. Bureaucratic requirements necessitate literally mounds of paperwork that can only be completed by expensive professional accountants. Second, taxes and fees leave little remaining from even the most encouraging of otherwise positive cash flow. Thus, now, in June 2001, as I review my latest bank report some seven years after our launch of Olim Creative Products, I marvel at how abundantly God has provided for this new company.

Hallelujah! The company is, indeed miraculously, finally profitable with a positive cash flow and has been so for almost a year. However, the road to this long-sought success was anything but smooth—the journey was an exercise in sanctification, humility, and in the end, a seemingly unending succession of profound disappointments, which, in His mercy and grace were at last turned to abundant joy.

I was absolutely certain I had been called out of my initial employment in Israel to fulfill what at first seemed like a clear vision. My understanding was that I was to do two things: first, I was to help my fellow new immigrants get settled in the Land by creating employment and by otherwise providing financial assistance; next, I was to take the good news out of Zion through the written and spoken word.

I also am certain that this Olim vision was and remains from the Lord. I knew then that I had been called to create a business to provide employment for the returning remnant of *olim* (immigrants) to Israel. The profits from this business were to be used to ever increase this business base and thus its corresponding employment of *olim*. It wasn't my *understanding* of the concept that was mistaken—it was rather my failure to take sufficient time to seek, hear and then respond to *His* plans for precisely *how* this vision was to be accomplished.

It was thus that Olim Creative Products, Ltd. was registered in early 1994 with a far too hastily adopted initial agenda to establish two new product lines: *Remembrance* Communion Wine, and *Awakening* Dead Sea Cosmetics. One of these new ventures has, after repeated trial and error, turned out to be from the Lord. The other apparently was not.

Even so, the Lord not only allowed me to forge on ahead without the benefit of His precise guidance, but He used my folly to teach and polish so that in the end, while I emerged a bit bruised and worn from the experience, I also grew in my understanding of His will for my life, and I took several hard but precious steps forward along the pathway of my sanctification.

What now I seek most to convey is the wonderful truth that through all of this, the good and the bad, He was ever with me, illuminating the way with His never ending array of signs, wonders and miracles.


During my earlier employment in Israel, I had overseen the marketing and distribution of a non-alcoholic, Israeli-produced communion grape juice that had been selling well to a small but growing international market. I wasn't therefore at all surprised that during this time I received several inquiries from potential "high Church" customers who desired to purchase a regular alcoholic communion wine from Israel. One of these was the German distributor of our grape juice product who visited me and my former employer for the express purpose of trying to persuade us to develop and export such an alcoholic product. While my former employer agreed with the economic good sense of offering such a new line, I could only acknowledge and respect his personal conviction that it would not be proper for him to do so. It was thus to answer this seemingly clear and as yet unfilled market need that the idea for *Remembrance* Communion Wine took root as one of the two launch products for my new company.

My initial research and contacts revealed that Barkan Wines, the second largest producer of Israeli wine, appeared to be the best prospect for supplying *Remembrance.* I had already been discussing the concept by phone with the general manager of Barkan. He was very interested, even excited about its prospects, since he had long been seeking a way to penetrate what he saw as a very large potential Christian market. We thus, during our most recent conversation, agreed to meet in his office at noon the following day when we would together taste and select an appropriate blend of wines for the new product and discuss several other aspects of the venture.

Since we had, up to now, not ventured far from Tiberias in our new car, Donna and I were thrilled that evening as we looked over the still unfamiliar road map of our new country to plan my next day's trip to Barkan.

I had been told that Barkan Wines was located in the Barkan Industrial Area, just across the so called "Green Line" in Judea. It was an out-of-the-way sort of place, right in the very heart of our new country, which I found with some difficulty and then circled on the map. In our still great innocence, neither Donna nor I gave a moment's thought to any potential danger there might be in traveling in Israel. After all, this was *our* country, protected by *our* military—in short, it just never entered our minds that I might be placing myself in extreme peril by following the old trip-planning axiom: "the shortest distance between two points is a straight line." It was thus quite innocently that I plotted a course from Tiberias to Barkan that took me right through the very heart of the so called "occupied territories." Thank God that Donna and I took time to pray together quite specifically just before I began my journey.

"O Lord," we prayed. "We ask your favor on this drive through the heartland of our beloved country. Protect Bob as he travels forth to serve you. Surround our new car with a band of your heavenly angels."

"And, Lord," I added, almost as an afterthought, "I ask that you help me to arrive at my appointment *on time.*"

We calculated it to be no more than a two-hour drive to Barkan. Thus, to make certain that I arrived on time for this important appointment, I left home at nine o'clock,  not two but three hours before the appointed noon meeting.

I didn't begin to realize the depth  of my great folly until I found myself stuck in a hopeless traffic jam in the town square right in the center of Jenin. Suddenly, my grave situation became crystal clear when my Israeli licensed-plated new car was instantly surrounded by a group of about twenty young Arabs, not one of whom looked even *slightly* friendly. Jenin was then and remains today one of the gravest hot beds of Palestinian terrorism in Israel. Even under the best of circumstances, it is anything but a safe place for a Jew.  At first, my concern was only for the untoward delay and the fact that it would now be unlikely that, even with the extra hour, I would make it to Barkan by noon. However, as my group of new Arab "friends" started rocking my car somewhat violently, keeping my business appointment suddenly became the least of my concerns.

"O my God!" I prayed. "What have I done?? Save me, O Lord!! Show me what I am to do!!" I beseeched my Creator for supernatural guidance as in the flesh I concluded that I would be most fortunate to get away from this place with a simple stoning.

As the  car-rocking grew more violent, without even the slightest conscious thought, I found myself  pressing the automatic window opening button. I then heard myself calmly addressing the young man who now thrust his head menacingly through my window, as his very close foul smelling breath along with my somehow amazingly subdued panic made me nauseated. "*Salaam,*" I warmly offered my one word of Arabic.

"What are *you* doing here?" my self-appointed interrogator and leader of my tormentors began in surprisingly good English, his voice a blend of incredulity and hostility.

I "listened" to my reply as if I were an observer rather than a participant in this conversation. "I'm so glad you came along," I said, sounding genuinely relieved. "I'm an American business-man—I'm afraid I have lost my way. Can you please tell me how to get from here to Barkan?"

My would-be assailant bought the ruse entirely. The sudden change in his countenance, from hostility to warm acceptance, was truly remarkable. He screamed a command to his associates who had continued to rock the car during our brief exchange. They stopped their intimidation at once and joined in their leader's dramatically changed approach towards this unusual "American businessman" in their midst.

"It may take a while for this traffic to start moving," my former would be assailant turned 'friend' advised, "but when it does, all you have to do is keep going straight. You will eventually see some signs pointing the way, but just remember to keep going straight."

"Thank you so much," I said, taking his extended hand through the open window.

"Have a nice day," he said, as he turned and walked away.

It was well over another half hour before the traffic in Jenin at last began to crawl its way out of the city. Yes, I noticed, there *were* many signs, most in Arabic, a few in Hebrew and not a sin-gle one in English. Worse still, along the way I encountered not one but two three-forked intersections, any direction from which could well have been considered "straight." In each case I took a deep breath, chose one of the three possible directions, then blindly forged ahead. Despite the sense that I was totally lost in hostile territory, here in the heart of Samaria as I looked about me, I was overwhelmed by the sheer beauty of the place. My mind was suddenly filled with scripture:

> *And I will bring them out from the peoples and gather them from the countries, and will bring them to their own land; I will feed them on the mountains of Israel, in the valleys and in all the inhabited places of the country.* (Ezek 34:13)

Then it dawned on me as I aimlessly drove along, this trip was no accident. I had not lost my way. No, this was God's wonderful way of giving me a close look at the very heart of the Land he had given to His Jewish people as an everlasting inheritance. This was *my* Land, I joyfully reflected! This is *not* Arab land, not one square inch, I cried out as I greatly rejoiced.

Still hopelessly lost after about another half hour of driving through this beautiful territory, I decided to stop at the first gas station I came across to ask further directions. I wasn't at all surprised when the attendant, seeing my Israeli yellow license plates, responded initially with considerable hostility.

"Do you speak English?" I asked, anticipating the blank silent-stare response.

"Sprechen Sie Deutsche?" I tried German, my almost workable second language.

"Yah!" the attendant replied warmly. "Ein Bishen."

I had followed the new directions provided by the attendant for more than yet another half hour. They had been more of the same. "Go straight ahead." I still didn't have a clue where I was, and I found myself once again beginning to become genuinely concerned.

It was then that I found my way suddenly blocked by two Israeli state policemen who stood in the middle of the road, and were flagging me down.

"Boy, am I glad to see you guys!" I greeted one of these presumed protectors through my open window.

"What are *you* doing here?" He asked incredulously. "Where do you think you are going?"

"I'm trying to get to Barkan," I responded sheepishly. "I've been told to just keep driving straight ahead—Is that right?"

"Straight ahead is *Shechem*," the officer responded. "Do you *like* your car? Do you want to keep *living?*" he added sarcastically.

"What do you mean?" I responded quite innocently.

"I *mean* if you drive another five kilometers straight ahead you will at the very least be stoned, your car destroyed—You could well be lynched!"

I was too stunned and grateful for my salvation to immediately respond.

The officer called out instructions to his colleague. Then, turning once again to me, he offered now warmly: "Come, my friend, we will make a sandwich with you as the meat and our two vans as the bread. We will lead you out of this wilderness. Just follow me and be patient; it will take awhile."

As promised, it did take awhile, at least another half hour as I guided my Subaru, now in the safekeeping of a police van both fore and aft as they led me over narrow, obviously seldom-traveled back roads through some of the most beautiful places I have ever seen. Finally the van in front pulled to the side of the road, and I stopped behind him and got out of my car to join its driver who had become my personal guide to presumed safety.

"Turn left here," he instructed, pointing to the small branch just ahead. "Follow this for about another thirty kilometers and you will come to a "Y" intersection. Bear right at this intersection, then go straight, and it will take you into Barkan. You should be there in an hour or so."

I thanked both police offers profusely for their life-saving assistance, then resumed my journey, praising the Lord as I went along. But I had not yet come to the end of this incredible saga.

As advertised, after about thirty kilometers, I came to the "Y" intersection. To this day I'm not sure why I was again so confused, but, be that as it may, instead of bearing to the right as I had been instructed, I went to the left. Fortunately, this compounding error did not lead me into any further danger. Instead, after about yet another half hour of winding up a very high mountain, I came to a small village at the top that just happened to have a hospital where two English speaking ambulance attendants gave me yet further directions to Barkan.

"You should have gone right at the 'Y' intersection, I was informed. "Retrace your steps, take the other direction, and you will be in Barkan in about an hour or so."

I was both more than a little relieved and embarrassed at my tardiness when at last I found myself driving about the rather large Barkan Industrial Area, looking, at first, without any success for the Barkan Winery.

Finally, after asking directions from two separate individuals, I found myself about to enter the office marked "General Manager."

I knew I was *terribly* late and as I took my host's extended hand in greeting, I prepared to apologize and explain my long delay. It was then that my eyes caught the large clock on the wall just behind his desk. I found myself totally speechless as I beheld the second hand of this clock sweeping twelve o'clock noon. Amazingly! Impossibly! Incredibly!  By the very hand of God, I was *precisely* on time! The Lord had answered  our prayer quite specifically. By some series of connected miracles He had shortened what had to have been about a five hour journey into three hours. I didn't even try to explain to my host what had happened. How could I, when I was still struggling in the depths of my being trying to explain it to myself. Instead, as planned, we immediately launched into our business discussion.

Once again, the Lord God of Israel had demonstrated Himself through His grace alone to be my bountiful provider, my never failing protector and the lifter of my head.

> *But You, O LORD, are a shield for me, my glory and the One who lifts up my head. I cried to the LORD with my voice, and He heard me from His holy hill. Selah I lay down and slept; I awoke, for the LORD sustained me.* (Ps 3:3-5)

As I drove home to Tiberias from Barkan, this time taking the longer, safe route along the Mediterranean coast, I couldn't stop marveling at how God had had His almighty hand upon me that day. Little did I then realize that His signs, wonders and miracles in my new life as a citizen of Israel had only just begun.

As for *Remembrance* Communion Wine, the new product was an excellent, not expensive, beautifully packaged offering. Inexplicably, however, we were not able to find a sufficient market for it to be continued as a regular product of our new company. Thus, after we sold out the initial production, mostly to local Churches, we sadly discontinued its production.

## Chapter Four

## "Thus Saith the Lord"

*And God said: "This is the sign of the covenant which I make between Me and you, and every living creature that is with you, for perpetual generations I set My rainbow in the cloud, and it shall be for the sign of the covenant between Me and the earth."(Gen 9:9-13)*

As we thus struggled in vain to establish *Remembrance* Communion Wine, we simultaneously worked to develop our new line of *Awakening* Dead Sea Cosmetics.

Everything seemed to be right on track as we negotiated with one of Israel's top manufacturers who agreed to produce an initial seven products for the Christian market under our own, nicely packaged private label.

To top this off, my brother Marty and his partner, Rob Hardwicke, who together operated a prospering marketing consultant business in Lafayette, California, expressed a desire to be our exclusive importer with the intention of establishing

*Awakening* and other Olim Creative products in the North American market. So we quickly discussed, negotiated, defined, then founded our importing company, Olim Industries of North America, Ltd.

Soon after this, Marty dropped his biggest account (wherein he was the marketing focal point for all Chilean produce exported to North America) so that he could apply most of his time to *Awakening*. Rob, a well-established public relations expert, immediately set to positioning *Awakening* in several niches within the American market.

There was, however, much to be learned on *both* sides of this new Olim venture. For my part, I found myself like a kid in a candy store wanting to try everything all at once. I unwisely committed the company to several other unrelated new product experiments, none of which proved more than just marginally profitable. Olim North America also got off to a roaring start in the *wrong* direction. Instead of introducing the *Awakening* product line into a ready-and-waiting, traditional, wholesale-retail market place, Marty and Rob opted to establish an elaborate multi-level marketing system which was difficult and costly to manage, a natural turn-off to much of the Christian market where it was largely directed, and worst of all, because of the complex and demanding multiple commission schedule involved, it drove end consumer prices to near prohibitive levels. In short, we had put our heads together and developed the best Dead Sea product line on the market, then postured ourselves so that our efforts couldn't possibly be a financial success.

Even so, in the midst of all our error, the Lord manifested Himself to show us that He was there, waiting to lead us when we were at last ready to listen.

Less than a month after we had launched *Awakening*, Donna

and I were attending a gathering in Tiberias of local believers and a group of American tourists from Kansas City. It was then and remains today a distinct pleasure for us to mingle with believers from the States. For us, these all too infrequent interfaces provide a sort of "sanity check" and a touch of our former home. It is a joy for us to discuss Israel, *aliyah,* and many of the unusual happenings that fill our lives as immigrants to the Land.

On this particular occasion, I found myself making eye contact with an otherwise average-looking gentleman who's piercing, bright blue eyes drew me to him like a spiritual magnet. "I have a word for you," he said simply, picking me out of the crowd.

Suddenly, virtually everyone in the visiting group reacted. "Gene Bacon has a word!" someone cried out, as if to alert anyone who had somehow managed not to pick up on what was to them an obviously important happening.

Within moments, I found myself face to face with Gene, who, I was later told, was a well known "Kansas City prophet." We were surrounded by members of his group who had gathered close so as not to miss a word of what they felt the Lord had to say to me through this representative. One of them held a microphone between us so as to capture the message on tape for later study.

Later, I transcribed the tape, and here, in part, is what this Kansas City prophet had for me from the Lord:

> And the Lord said, "It is my vision and the scope of it that you now have," says the Lord, "it is not what it shall be because I shall give you yet more," says the Lord God, "and not only will you sell products and distribute products that others will give, but I will give you products of your own," says the Lord, "and I will bring you inventors," saith God.

"I shall give you products that shall be found no place but here," saith the Lord. "And this will be the only place to get them." And God says, "you are going to go to other countries." And the Lord says, "I want you to know that it is not just for Israel, but for Christians in other countries as well....

"You will travel and you will be the one who lays your hands upon them and will impart the vision and the anointing that I have given unto you," saith the Lord. "—I will show you that no obstacle that comes before you will be able to stand," says the Lord, "but I will show you that this is of me.

"—I have shown you something; you are going to impart this vision even unto others—I see your brother doing a tremendous business in America distributing what God will bring in—and God is going to bless this man. He is going to have to build another warehouse; God is going to give him space to store the products that are going to be sent. This is my doing; this is my work," saith God.

"This is being done by the hand of God, and all will see it and no man will be able to touch it. No man will be able to put his hand upon it and to withdraw from it and to detract from it. But this is mine," saith the Lord. "I will watch over it. I will protect it," saith the Lord.

The Lord says, "I want you to have rest. I want you to be worry free. I want you to be free of fear," saith the Lord. "You let me take care of everything," saith God. "You just put one foot in front of the other and take a step as I direct your step," says the Lord."

Several weeks following my encounter with Gene Bacon, I was all the more astounded when the Lord crossed my path with that of a most unusual visitor, a gentleman in his mid-forties from the United States, who said he had been directed by the Lord to bring me a confirming word regarding my call to Israel.

I had neither met nor heard of this person before. I knew him only by what he told me: that his name was Reuben and that he was an "official" in the Full Gospel Businessmen's International. He also reported to me that he had a special call as an "apostle to Israel."

I must confess that I was somewhat skeptical about his anointing, that is, until he laid hands on me in prayer and gave me the following confirming input which has proven over time and through subsequent events to have been from the Lord. In summary, here is what he said:

> You are not called to be a pastor, but rather a teacher and a facilitator. Your ministry is to bring the word out of Zion to the nations. You will travel far and wide, teaching many the truth about Israel and its true relationship to the world. You will send the word out from Zion and you will speak in many distant places.

> The Lord will give your company products that are unique to Israel, and you will eventually have great business success, the proceeds of which will bring great blessings to Israel, the Jewish people and to the Church.

The first six months or so of our Israeli corporate activity was the most demanding time of my entire professional experience. I was physically and emotionally exhausted from the effort, and Donna was equally drained by her constant figurative and often literal holding of my hand as I muddled my way through the many challenges of my new existence: six days a week, each regularly consisting of twelve to fourteen arduous hours.

It was because of this that on the occasion of our thirty-fifth wedding anniversary in late January' we made a long weekend reservation at a plush resort hotel in Eilat, at the extreme southern end of Israel on the shore of the Gulf of Eilat. Little did I realize as we drove toward this much needed rest that the Lord would use this occasion to manifest Himself in several genuinely remarkable ways.

I really hadn't given it much thought, but it was obviously the Lord who had caused me to bring along several samples of our new *Awakening* products. Donna particularly loved the cosmetic products, especially the body lotion and the shampoo, but as I stepped into the shower on the first evening of our holiday, I noticed the jar of our "Authentic Dead Sea Black Mud" that I had included with the other items and wondered why in the world I had been led to do so.

The Lord soon answered my unspoken question. As I stood there enjoying the luxury of a strong massage shower, He gave me an instruction that was equally clear as it was puzzling. "Put Dead Sea mud on your entire scalp. Cover every bit of the top of your head with it. Leave it there for thirty minutes, then shower it off. Do this every day." Since He didn't bother to explain the purpose of this seemingly bizarre undertaking, I came up short in being able to provide Donna with a reasonable explanation when I presented myself to her a few minutes later adorned with my first Dead Sea mud bonnet.

Not surprisingly, her first reaction was hilarity. "What have you done to your head??" she exclaimed as she nearly collapsed in a fit of laughter.

My only available recourse was to tell her the simple facts of God's message and my unquestioning obedience. This proved quite sufficient for us both as we pondered about what God might have in mind while we waited for my thirty minute treatment time to expire. After this, I returned to the shower to remove my black mud cap, we dressed and then enjoyed our first dinner out in several weeks.

Our mini-vacation flew away far too quickly, and we relished its every minute. A mini-sailing cruise on the Gulf in a private charter; eating all meals out in one gourmet restaurant after the next; just simply relaxing: all of it had been wonderful. Even the weather had been perfect, which wasn't an unusual thing this time of year at the southern tip of Israel. What was unusual were the threatening black clouds that began to fill the sky to the north just about the time we began our normally six-hour drive home to Tiberias. What turned out to be a severe winter storm started slowly, then, quite uncharacteristically, the rain poured out from heaven in torrents accompanied by violent claps of thunder and nearby streaks of lightning.

Donna has an enviable propensity to nap on even the shortest drives. This was a long trip following a wonderful and very busy weekend. It thus didn't surprise me to see her drift off in the seat next to me as the intensity of the winter storm began to ease.

Looking fondly at this lovely partner of our now thirty-five years together, I once again marveled as I often do at the depths of my love for her—indeed my one-flesh dependence upon her for so many of the aspects of my life. At once, I was filled with happiness, joy and fulfillment, and I began to quietly pray in the spirit a prayer of thanksgiving for all the Lord had done and was still apparently doing in our very blessed lives here in the Land to which He had called us.

Then, when we were about five miles from the southernmost end of the Dead Sea, the Lord spoke to me in the midst my prayer in His wonderful unmistakable confirming way: "I am going to give you a rainbow, my son, as a sign that I am with you in all that I have called you to do."

I glanced about the sky around us. Although the rain had entirely stopped, it was solid gray. These were not the conditions for a rainbow, and after I had looked for the promised phenomenon for several minutes to no avail, my mind began to drift, and I soon found myself once again in prayer.

I had just about put the promise of a rainbow entirely out of my mind, that is, until we rounded a bend in the narrow two-lane highway and beheld the beginnings of the Dead Sea. Suddenly, the beauty of what I saw before my eyes literally took my breath away.

"There it is!!" I cried out in a loud voice.

"There is *what?*" Donna exclaimed, having been rudely awakened from her sound sleep.

"The rainbow!!" I cried out. "God's promised rainbow!! Don't you see it??"

"I don't see *anything,*" she said yawning, trying to wake up.

I followed the direction of her gaze and saw that my instructions had been inadequate. "No!" I corrected. "Look *down,* right above the surface of the water!"

"Praise God!!" she exclaimed in awe. "It's beautiful! Incredibly beautiful! I've never seen anything like it!"

Nor had I. The rainbow we beheld was perfect. Each color band was precisely defined. And instead of arching up in the usual elevated bow, this display extended in an almost straight, ever so subtly arched line, just above the surface of the sea. It began quite definitively on the Israeli shore just a few hundred yards from our present location, and it extended with perfect clarity all the way across the glimmering, now sun-bathed body of azure blue water to the Jordanian side.

No sooner had Donna announced her confirming recognition of this amazing phenomenon than, in the same startling manner in which it had appeared, it suddenly vanished before our very eyes.

Yes, the Lord God of Israel *was* with us, and we didn't have long to wait until we experienced yet another manifestation of His astounding, saving presence.

The respite in the winter storm had been all too brief, orchestrated it would seem so that we might have our truly blessed rainbow. Immediately after we had beheld this wonderful gift, the sky opened up again and the downpour resumed.

As we reached about the halfway point along the Dead Sea, we suddenly came to a complete halt near the front of a growing line of bumper to bumper stalled traffic.

After a few minutes of no forward progress, I got out of the car and hurried through the continuing downpour to the front of the line to investigate. I quickly discovered the cause of our delay. One of the many *wadis* (gullies) descending from the surrounding mountains was overflowing with a torrent of the collected downpour, and the sheer force of this rushing water had taken about thirty meters of the asphalt highway with it as it had coursed on into the sea below. There were now highway patrol cars on both sides of the large washout, and as I watched, one of them from our side boldly, if not foolishly, decided to test the situation by attempting to cross to the other side. No sooner had the police car entered the water than it sank two or three feet before its wheels found a purchase on the unstable gravel bottom. Finally, fighting the raging current that seemed determined to push this lonely intruder into the sea, the police car managed to make it to the other side.

In my mind, I quickly concluded that the road would remain

closed until the flood had subsided, no matter how long this might take. We were, I determined as I headed back to our car to explain the situation, going to be stuck in this place for at least several hours. However, to my sheer amazement, just as I finished explaining all this to Donna, the car in front of us began, inexplicably, to move forward. I couldn't believe my eyes. The police were directing traffic to cross the rushing torrent one car at a time.

"Oh, Sweetheart! I'm frightened. Let's turn around and go back!" Donna echoed my own emotions as we edged forward, watching as each car in front of us, in turn, took its own plunge into the now raging water and struggled to the other side.

"I'm afraid it's too late for that," I replied, noting that there was no way for us to physically turn around on what had now narrowed to only one lane. It was either that we stop and simply refuse to cross, thus compounding the situation, or that we take a deep breath and take our own plunge into the rushing torrent before us.

The policeman on the other side signaled for me to proceed. We prayed aloud in our growing terror—then I plunged our Subaru into the rushing, muddy water. It seemed to take forever for our wheels to find a purchase on the bottom and when they did, it was insufficient to hold against the pressure of the water that decidedly pushed us downstream, closer and closer to the place where it perilously dropped off into the Dead Sea.

"Help us!! Help us O Lord!!" we both cried out as I struggled to regain control against the terribly strong current.

By the time we at last began making forward progress, the water had already reached about halfway up our doors. Yet, we *were* moving forward, and miraculously, within moments we did, just barely, make it to the other side. We were the *last* car to do so that evening. Wisely, the police determined to close the road right after they had observed our nearly disastrous passage.

One evening in the early spring of 1996, I was sitting on the couch in our salon reading the Friday *Jerusalem Post*. As she often did, Donna approached me from behind, put her arms around my neck and lovingly began to massage my shoulders.

"Sweetheart!" she exclaimed at the wonder of her discovery. "You are *growing hair!!*"

I had already observed during the past two or three weeks that there had been signs of new stubble growing on my mostly bald crown, but I just hadn't been bold enough to make the declaration of this surprising happening.

"I think it's the Dead Sea mud," I replied enthusiastically. "I've been using it each day these past few weeks, just like the Lord instructed - this must be what He had in mind."

"Are you trying to tell me that Dead Sea mud grows hair?" Donna went on, as if questioning her own eyes and touch as she ran her fingers over my undeniable crop of new stubble.

"How else can you explain it?" I replied. "I'm going to fax Marty and Rob about this. Just maybe the Lord is giving us an amazing new product. You know, this goes right along with the Gene Bacon prophecy."

My crop of new hair continued to increase over the next several weeks as I awaited some response from Marty. He called me one evening to express his excitement about my apparent, incredible discovery.

"This is the most exciting new thing since the discovery of the wheel!" he nearly shouted at me over the six thousand or so miles between us, as if better trying to make his point. "It's genuinely amazing! I'm growing hair too! "There could be a *fortune* in this for all of us!!"

"What's next?" I asked, trying not to explode with my own growing excitement as I envisioned the potential of establishing a huge tax free fund to help new olim get settled in the Land.

"I've already talked to one of the leading patent attorneys in

San Francisco," my ecstatic brother replied. "He tells me that we need to test this stuff scientifically by conducting some reasonable, medically supervised study of some appropriate number of bald and balding men. Then, if the data from this test warrants, and I'm sure it will, we next file for a U.S. patent."

"How do you patent something *natural* like this?" I asked, being almost totally uninformed about such matters.

"The patent attorney told me it isn't going to be easy, and it may take a very long time, but there is precedent for just this sort of thing."

A simple "Wow!" was the only response I could muster.

"Don't worry about anything!" Marty continued. "Rob is already putting together the beginnings of a medically supervised trial—you can be sure we will stay right on top of this!"

Some six months later, I found myself sitting at a huge mahogany table in the luxuriously appointed penthouse conference room of one of the most prestigious patent law firms in San Francisco. Marty, Rob and I had spent the past hour discussing in detail the results of our medically supervised testing of what we were now calling "HTM" (an acronym for Hair Treatment Method). In short, all present were astounded at the results of this survey. All but four of the twenty-three test participants, ranging in age from 23 to 59, had benefited to some significant, measurable extent after having used HTM for the first five months of a one-year trial. In short, more than 70% of the participants had grown hair—some now had full crops of it growing on what had once been entirely bald, or nearly bald pates.

Further, there were already clear indications that HTM not only grew hair but that it also greatly curtailed hair loss. Moreover, as strange as it seemed, this amazing natural substance also had a wonderful impact on hair grooming. Those who used it universally commented on how it made their hair much softer and easier to control while giving it a rich, gleaming, healthy appearance.

The implications of this were clear: HTM also had great potential as a product to be used by women. In short, the results were so impressive that our attorneys had determined that we already had sufficiently compelling data to submit our patent application without further delay.

"What are the chances for this application being approved?" I asked the two attorneys, adding a suddenly sobering note to our otherwise heady conversation.

"Quite frankly," one of the two answered without hesitation, "the chances for approval are no better than fifty-fifty."

"How long will it take for the patent office to make a determination?" I continued.

"It could take as long as a year, even as long as two or even three years if they turn us down the first time and we decide to appeal." He hesitated for a moment, then went on. "Guys, to be honest, in our opinion you are sitting on top of a potential gold mine, but your chances of getting to the mother lode are quite uncertain. In any event, it is going to be a very long and hard row to hoe. In short, our advice is that you let us handle all this, and to the extent that you can, put it out of your minds and get on with your other business."

One of the two attorneys stopped me at the door as we were leaving the conference room at the end of the meeting. "Bob, please forgive me if I am out of line for asking this, but how is it that you came to try this stuff on your head in the first place?"

"I don't mind you asking at all." I replied. "The fact is, the Lord God of Israel called me home to the Land and He has been leading me by the hand ever since I responded to His call. This may be hard for you to believe, but He personally *told* me to do this."

As we shook hands in departure, the attorney made no effort

to conceal the stream of tears that were coursing down his cheeks.

The patent application was officially filed on November 19, 1996. As instructed, from that point on Marty, Rob and I did our best to put HTM out of our minds and to get on with the many other things we had on our respective plates. However, the three of us found it impossible to do so. This new, genuinely amazing, potential product was never far from our thoughts. Fortunately, and miraculously we didn't have long to wait! Once again, the Lord intervened.

"Bob!" Marty almost shouted over the phone after waking me in the wee hours of the morning on April 2, 1997. The urgency and excitement in my brother's voice snapped me from my deep slumber into full wakefulness.

"You're not going to *believe* this!" Marty continued. "I just got a call from our attorney. Even he doesn't believe it!!"

"Believe *what*?" I ventured.

"Bob—our patent has been *granted!* Not only that, it was granted with no exceptions!"

"How could that be?" I asked. "This was supposed to take at least a year, and it has only been five months?"

The trembling in Marty's voice was obvious. "Not only is this the shortest response period ever experienced by our attorneys who are the biggest in this field, but our application was person- ally walked through the system by the head person in this branch of the Patent Office. As far as our attorneys know, this has never happened before, certainly not with any of the many thousands of applications they have handled."

"Do you kind of get the idea that God is in this thing?" I almost whispered, verbalizing my own profound amazement.

"How could it be anything else?" Marty replied.

Several months had passed since our patent had been miraculously granted when I received another of what had become progressively more despondent, telephoned progress reports from my brother.

"That's the last of them," Marty sighed dejectedly as he reported the results of his most recent in a series of meetings with top executives of America's largest pharmaceutical firms. "They said essentially the same thing as all the others. In short, they think we have a great potential product but they have no interest in exploring it further at this time."

"Did they give the same reasons we've already heard?" I asked.

"Almost exactly." Marty replied. "Their biggest concern is that it would be almost impossible to isolate the element or combination of elements in the basic natural substance that is responsible for the great results we've gotten. They are also very concerned that the basic substance must surely vary in content from place to place around the Dead Sea. So, who is to guarantee that the results would be anything like standard or in any way dependable."

"That was *all* of it?" I asked.

"Oh no, lest I forget," Marty added sarcastically. "They expressed the same old 'if it was not invented here, like, for example *Rogaine,* we aren't going to touch it' attitude. Let's face it; these folks are organic chemists. If they can't make it or copy it they don't want to mess with it."

"Okay," I replied, trying to mask the depth of my disappointment. "So much for the several-million-dollars-up-front strategy. The Olim Foundation is just going to have to wait a bit longer. God's timing is God's timing. He can't be rushed! Nuu?? So what do we do next?"

Marty didn't hesitate, even with some of his irrepressible excitement returning to his voice. "We market *HTM* right along with the rest of the *Awakening* line. It should attract a lot of attention as our most unique offering. We'll offer it with a sister product we'll call *Ultimate Hair Treatment for Women*. You know," Marty began to sound once again like the inveterate marketer he was, "this is going to take a lot longer, but in the end, we will probably find ourselves further ahead by doing it all ourselves."

## Chapter Five

## A Home of Our Own

*Return to your own house, and tell what great things God has done for you.* (Luke 8:39a)

Amnon's announcement came as a sudden shock. He had a crushing financial problem and had decided to sell our apartment as a source of much needed cash. He stopped by one evening to tell us of his decision and to ask if we were interested in buying this place, we had come to so love, before he put it on the open market.

"I just don't see where we are going to find the money to swing this," I lamented to Donna after we had put Amnon off, telling him we would think it over and give him a call. "Maybe we should just continue renting on a month to month basis until we either find some more money or until Amnon sells the apartment to someone else!"

"Sweetheart! This is *our* apartment: Amnon *isn't* going to sell it to anyone else!! The Lord provided us with a beautiful new car and He is going to provide us with enough money to buy this apartment!"

"Who am I to argue with such faith?" I replied. "But the fact is, we need quite a *lot* of money we don't happen to have at the moment."

"How much?"

"The way I have it figured, a mere *thirty-six thousand* dollars more than we can get our hands on right now!" I replied.

"Well, let's just keep praying and we'll see where we are when you get back from your upcoming business trip to the States."

I was about to depart on a short visit the focus of which was to meet with potential investors who had shown an interest in my new company. "The Lord will do what the Lord will do," I replied.

" Indeed He will," Donna agreed.

"I'm really looking forward to speaking at Beth Simcha," I added. "It was so nice of Frank to set up a sort of homecoming for me."

"Be careful not to bug him too much about making *aliyah*," Donna warned teasingly, knowing full well that *aliyah* for Frank and all of the other ethnic Jews in the congregation would be the fervent subject of my message.

One of the great benefits of military retirement is the privilege of using cost free "space available" travel. When there is an otherwise open seat on a military aircraft anyplace in the world, retirees can claim it on a first come first served basis. I had determined that there were usually two scheduled military flights a week to Israel from Germany, en route to the United States, and since money was a major consideration, I decided to give this free travel system a try.

"We have a C-5 scheduled into Ben Gurion Airport this afternoon, Colonel," the sergeant at the "Space-A" desk at Ramstein Air Base, Germany informed me by phone. "It should be arriving around 1400 hours, but just to make sure, give us a call in a couple of hours to confirm that it has departed as scheduled."

I was greatly disappointed to learn, two hours later, when I called back, that the Tel Aviv leg of this particular flight had been canceled  because of technical problems and had it already departed non-stop to Dover Air Force Base, Delaware. The "Space A" sergeant at Ramstein suggested that I establish contact with Laufer Aviation at Ben Gurion Airport. Laufer, he informed me, was their agent  that provided all passenger services and were well informed about potential travel opportunities.

Thus, about an hour after I had been informed that there would be no flight that day, I called Laufer to see if they had any information about flights later in the week.

"Can you get here in two hours?" the Laufer representative asked, immediately after I had explained my travel requirements. "We have a C-5 from Ramstein  in the landing pattern right now en route to Dover. He'll be on the ground for about two hours, and you would be the only passenger."

"Was this a scheduled flight?" I asked incredulously.

"No, sir," the Laufer agent responded. "It just sort of appeared out of nowhere. We didn't know about it until they called in for landing clearance a few minutes ago."

"I'm on my way!" I replied excitedly, as I grabbed my still-packed suitcase and called for Donna to drive me to the airport.

Our trip to Ben Gurion took exactly two hours.  I was met by a Laufer agent who hurried me into a waiting staff car that quickly drove took me to the huge transport aircraft with prominent "U.S. Air Force" markings.

"Welcome aboard, Colonel Fischer," the crew chief greeted me warmly.

"It's good to be 'home'," I replied, returning his salute, trying to hold back the tears that were unabashedly streaming down my cheeks.

The flight to Dover was wonderful and without incident, as was the "Space A" flight back to Israel via Ramstein.

The Lord has a wonderful way of setting up His miracles. He *knew*, even before He formed the universe, that we would be needing a large sum of money to buy our apartment. His provision for this need began toward the end of my Air Force career, when I got involved in a short period of highly speculative, small capital outlay investments in "penny stocks." My very aggressive penny stock broker in Denver called one or more of our growing group of staff officer investors each day with an amazing assortment of investment opportunities, each of which seemingly had some possibility, however minuscule, of producing great financial return. After several months of active trading, it turned out that I had, thankfully, about broken even for all my efforts, but it had been a lot of fun and the source of much good fellowship with my fellow investors.

When I left the Air Force to hurriedly take up my new employment with Boeing in Seattle, I had quite undeliberately retained only one of these penny stock holdings in my now otherwise depleted Denver portfolio. While my twenty thousand shares in Pantheon Industries were at the time worth all of the 1 cent per share I had paid for them, and as far as I knew, had no immediate growth potential, I nevertheless had retained them.

Even now, some ten years after I had made this highly speculative investment, I still occasionally checked to see if there had been any movement in its value. I made such a check about a week before I was to depart on my previously mentioned trip to the United States.

To my *great* surprise, the quote had suddenly, and with no supporting news, moved from where it had not budged from its seemingly permanent 1 cent, to 10 cents per share. I excitedly decided to sell all my holdings and take a nice profit that would greatly help us raise the money we still needed to buy the apartment. However, the still quiet voice whispered—"*Not yet!*"

The day before I climbed on the C-5 for headed for Dover, I

called my broker again. Further fueling my growing excitement, he reported that the stock was now up to 15 cents per share and there appeared to be more potential in this sudden, yet still unexplained upswing.

I called him again, right after I arrived at Dover.

He reported that the stock had already peaked out, amazingly, at more than $6 per share, however, that it was now beginning to quickly decline. Excitedly, I gave him an order to sell *all* my shares. He advised me, though, that he could immediately sell only ten thousand shares since the remaining ten thousand were not yet registered. I told him to register and then sell them as quickly as he could.

The next morning, after I arrived, via a commercial flight, in Seattle, I again contacted my broker. He had managed to sell the registered ten thousand shares for a price that after commissions and taxes yielded precisely $36,000, the exact additional amount we needed to buy our apartment. The stock, he further reported to his amazement, had again immediately retreated to the 1 cent level, before the other ten thousand shares could be registered.

Praise the Lord! We bought the apartment immediately upon my return to Tiberias.

And so it was, at the end of our second year as citizens of Israel, that we found ourselves greatly blessed with a wonderful new car and an apartment that far exceeded our greatest expectations. Thus we felt called to use these great gifts as much as possible for the glory of Him from whom they had come. Towards this end, we were led to establish an intercessory prayer group that quickly grew to about sixteen local believers who met in our home each Wednesday evening.

After one such wonderful, spirit-filled evening, when Donna and I had bid our guests goodnight, we returned to our comfortable chairs on the main *meerpeset* where all of us had spent the past two hours in one of the most Holy Spirit filled praise and worship sessions of our experience. Just minutes before, we had been singing, dancing and rejoicing in this place as we looked out over the beautiful city of Tiberias, the full moon illuminating the Golan Heights  and the star-filled blue-black heavens, all of this reflected in the mirror-still surface of the Sea of Galilee. It was then, as we sat there next to one another, hold-ing hands like newlyweds, filled to overflowing with our  shared joy, reveling in the complete spiritual perfection of this wonder-ful moment, that the Lord once again determined to reassuringly manifest Himself in our presence. I said nothing  when I first saw it. Instead, I blinked my eyes several times to make certain that they weren't playing tricks on me. When I was sure that this was real, I looked to Donna for confirmation.

"Sweetheart," I almost whispered. "Look in the chair right in front of us, the one pushed in right at the head of the table." I pointed to the large, oblong- shaped  table and the strange object that had caught my amazed attention that appeared to be seated on the nearest chair. "Do you see what I'm talking about?"

"Yesss!" she replied in her own near whisper. "It looks like a golden eye. Like the golden eye of a large bird, sitting there star-ing at us."

"I think it's a dove," I conjectured, then immediately caught myself. "But how could that be? Doves don't roost on chairs. And besides, there were bunches of people rollicking about all over this place just minutes ago. There is *no way* any dove or any bird would be sitting on a chair looking at us like this," I proclaimed, underscoring my own disbelief.

"Why don't you go look at it?" Donna suggested the obvious. "Maybe it's hurt or something?"

I rose slowly from my chair and took the one large stride that separated us from this mysterious visitor. Kneeling down, I could see with certainty that this was indeed a very large and beautiful dove. Assuming it must have been injured since it didn't immediately take flight, I reached down to gently touch it. Just as my fingers made contact, the beautiful, heaven sent creature leaped into the air and flew into the night.

*And the Holy Spirit descended in bodily form like*
*a dove...* (Luke 3:22a)

The Lord blessed us and our new home even further in another lovely way one evening soon after we had closed on the transaction and the apartment had officially and joyfully become our own. Both of us have always loved animals, and during our own childhoods and the time when our three daughters were growing up, we never went long without the intimate company of at least one family pet, each in turn, so it seemed, more precious and more greatly loved than any of the long list of its predecessors.

While Donna and I were equally fond of dogs and cats, the unavoidable logistics of living in a fifth floor penthouse apartment, made a cat and its convenient litter box, greatly preferable to a dog with its requisite frequent outings to the street below. We were thus delighted when one of our local friends offered us one of several Siamese kittens from the latest litter her own beautiful female had recently provided. We gratefully selected one of the female kittens , and were scheduled to pick her up in just another week when she would be mature enough to wean.

"You know, it really seems a shame for us not to adopt a wild kitten from one of the local garbage dumpster colonies," I commented soon after we had settled on bringing a genuine purebred into our family.

I was referring to the literally millions of undomesticated cats of every color, size, breed and conceivable combination thereof that reside, and there subsist upon the refuse of every Israeli kitchen, in countless large metal garbage repositories liberally scattered along every street throughout the entire country. Most Israelis simply ignore these ever present "garbage-can-cat" colonies and their many wild feline residents. Some few, particularly fervent animal lovers, take time to separate their edible garbage from the rest and leave it outside the dumpsters for more easy access by these poor, often starving creatures. Other, thankfully few, cat haters, torment them as if they were vermin, even worse, some municipalities occasionally set out poisoned bait for them so as to reduce their numbers when they grow too numerous.

"Sweetheart!" Donna beckoned on that fateful, cold and rainy, late winter evening. "Would you be a dear and go get us a loaf of bread at the *makolet*?"

"Sure," I replied, looking forward to the short outing, not realizing that it held in store for us something much more precious than a simple loaf of bread.

I caught sight of the poor little, near-dead creature sitting in the rain against the wall of an abandoned building right across the street from our apartment. Since I had to go that way in any event, I ventured closer, thinking for sure this singular coal-black, obviously very young wild kitten would scramble away as I approached. Not so. To my amazement, the tiny black ball of fur inexplicably remained in its place, even as I stooped down to have a closer look. Sadly, as I could easily observe, this poor creature was very ill indeed. Both of its infected eyes were sealed shut with mucus, and it was soaking wet and shivering. Gingerly, I picked it up and held it close to my face, and it began to purr. Then, getting quite personal, I made a quick investigation and found that this was most likely a male.

"*No!*" I proclaimed almost audibly, as I returned the kitten to its former place against the wall and hurried off to the *makolet.*

I took my time  going and coming, and even lingered around the small convenience store for a few extra minutes longer than necessary, trying to kill time. Surely, I reasoned, the kitten would be gone by the time I returned, I tried to convince myself. But in my heart I already knew I was hooked, and upon this realization, I rushed to the place where I had left this very sick little creature, hoping against hope that he would still be there, now genuinely fearing that in my folly he might be gone.

"Praise the Lord," I exclaimed as I was filled with a surge of joy when I discovered  he was still there, sitting exactly as I had left him, blind and shivering in the rain. I held him a bit longer this time, and he thanked me by increasing the volume of his happy, now even contented purring.

"*Nooo!*" I proclaimed, this time audibly, as I again, although much more reluctantly than before, returned him to his place and hurried back home to tell Donna about the experience.

"I'll tell you what," she said prophetically after I had quickly told her of my experience, "if he is still there when you go back, bring him home. He is obviously the cat the Lord has for us."

We took the sickly kitten to a local veterinarian the next morning. After his close examination the vet suggested that we keep our foundling for a few weeks, and if he was still alive after that time, then we could get on with giving him shots and perhaps seeing to his other several health problems.

And so it was that Tiberias the cat (whom we call "Teever," short for the Hebrew, *Teveriah* ) became an incredibly dear member of our family.

Had either Donna or I been given the opportunity to choose a cat of any size, sex, color or breed, the very last on either of our lists would have been a huge (now sixteen pounds), black (with Morris orange undercoating and two white spots) male with one shrunken, still undeveloped eye. Now, as we recall the overwhelming joy and love Teever has brought into our lives  these past eight years, we never cease to marvel at how wonderfully and lovingly the Lord  provided us with the pet of *His* choosing, the sorriest of all creatures in the eyes of many, instead of a purebred of our own earlier selection.

Teever has it all: very high intelligence, beauty (in the eyes of at least two who behold him) and cunning, along with a very fetching, inborn street smartness drawn from the myriad generations of his undomesticated forebears.

Mostly though, his greatest attraction is his constant, genuinely perceptible outpouring of both  gratitude and  love, which of course is returned in kind by the two human devotees whom he adopted.

## Chapter Six

## A New Tomb in a Garden

*Now in the place where He was crucified there was a garden, and in the garden a new tomb in which no one had yet been laid.* (John 19:41)

Reuven Efraim Schmalz is an *oleh* (immigrant) from Los Angeles, who came to Israel in the early 1970s with his wife Bethie to defend Zionism against its many enemies. His emigration was America's loss and Israel's gain. Reuven is one of the most multi-talented, gifted persons I have ever known. He is also my close and dear friend. The Lord first brought us together in early 1995 to do great things for His Glory. Some of these things have already unfolded—I know in my spirit that there are many more yet to come.

Reuven, although not formally educated beyond high school, is, in my view, a brilliant biblical historian. His lifelong study of the Nazarenes, the first Jewish believers in Yeshua, arguably makes him an authority on this most important, foundational period in the history of the Christian Church. It was Reuven that set me to writing for the Lord when he encouraged me to collaborate with him on our first book, *The Messianic Seal of the Jerusalem Church*, published in 1999. Reuven authored Part One of this two-part book, a brilliant history of the time leading up to the formation of the first Messianic synagogue established by James the Just on Mount Zion right after the ascension of His brother, Yeshua.

While Reuven is a gifted writer and unique, self-educated historian, he is also a greatly gifted sculptor, and it is through this, his unique artistic talent, that I came to meet him. Reuven had created a number of sculpted biblically oriented works and was looking for a way to market them. He couldn't have been a better candidate for me to work with in my quest to fulfill the vision of Olim Creative Products. Our mutual needs were the genesis of a solid working relationship and mutual admiration that have already endured for seven years. While our early collaborative efforts to develop marketable products met with a modicum of financial success, God opened a door of great importance to us both nearly three years after we began our professional association.

In February 1998, I received an inquiry from the director of the Upper Room, Inc. in Northern Kentucky. They were revitalizing the "Garden of Hope," a biblical tourist attraction that featured an exact replica of the Garden Tomb in Jerusalem and were looking for items that they might import from Olim Creative Products to sell in their gift shop on the site.

Donna and I visited the Garden Tomb in Jerusalem soon after our arrival in the Land. It was a *momentous* experience. The first time I entered this sacred place, believed by a very large segment of the Church to be the place where Yeshua rose from the dead, I was nearly overcome by an awesome, glorious spiritual presence.

Subsequently, each of the many times I have returned to this place over the years, I have never failed to experience a spiritual reconfirmation: I *know*—this indeed *is* the place.

I have only come to recently understand that this, my early, intense drawing to the Garden Tomb, was no accident. This sacred place and my relationship with it were to have extremely important ramifications several years later—ramifications that reach far beyond those initial product development needs of 1998. (While I had no way of understanding it then, this, my first drawing to the Garden Tomb, was a divinely established connection that would reach into this very moment in the year 2001 as I prayerfully prepare to write the *After Word* of my third book that you are now holding in your hands.)

It was thus, in 1998 in response to this inquiry from Kentucky, that the Lord immediately put an idea in my mind with such intensity that I could think of nothing else until I started the wheels rolling towards its fruition. First, I called Reuven.

"Do you suppose you could sculpt a hand- sized, near perfect three-dimensional replica of the Garden Tomb?" I asked, already anticipating his excited answer.

"Of course I can!" he replied. "Do you have a market for such a thing?"

It took several weeks of concentrated effort for the Garden Tomb model to emerge. We began with an all day visit to the site in Jerusalem where Reuven literally climbed all over the sacred place, examining and measuring it from every conceivable perspective. All the while, as he made his intense study, he instructed me to photograph the place from the many precise locations he chose. Subsequently, I provided Reuven with a set of enlarged prints, which pictured the tomb in the exact size of our envisioned model.

Using a set of calipers, Reuven, with amazing skill and craftsmanship, managed to create a three-dimensional model, perfect in every detail including the direction of the chisel marks, which he casually observed "were made by two different sculptors: one who was left-handed, the other right-handed."

The product that emerged, reproduced by Bethie from silicon rubber molds, has been wonderfully successful. During its three-year history many have been sold at the Garden Tomb Gift Shop, and in other places in Israel. Thus, this divinely inspired offering has not only become the mainstay of Olim Creative Products, Ltd., but it has also helped immensely to keep Reuven and his family financially afloat.

Sadly, after only one small initial shipment of our new product to "The Garden of Hope" in Northern Kentucky, spiritual warfare had its way, and the reopened Garden Tomb replica was once again closed to the public. This, however, did not in any way impact the Garden Tomb Gift Shop staff in Jerusalem, who excitedly test-marketed the product. None of us were surprised that it was immediately well received by many of the legions of Christian tourists who visit the place each year, and it has continued to be a success even in these terrible times of greatly diminished tourism to Israel due to the now long-standing and ongoing *intifada.*

But the Garden Tomb model was only a beginning.


Although I had noticed the three-part symbol comprised of the menorah, the star of David and the fish, I had never given it much thought until one day in mid-1998 when I happened to be engaged in a casual conversation with Eric Morey, General Manager of The Galilee Experience, an anointed business, owned and operated by believers in Tiberias. In retrospect, it was the Lord's timing that brought my latent curiosity to the surface.

"Eric," I inquired, "what can you tell me about this most interesting symbol? Does it have any historical significance, or did some clever person just dream it up in modern times?"

"I'm not really certain," Eric replied forthrightly, "but I know whom you can ask:  Ludwig Schneider, a German believer who lives in Jerusalem."

"Really?" I replied with growing interest. "What is his connection to all this?"

"All I can tell you is that Terri (Eric's wife) and Ludwig's wife are casual friends. Anyway, Terri told me that the Schneiders have several supposedly ancient artifacts bearing this symbol. In fact, the Schneiders have copyrighted the symbol as the logo of their publication, *Israel Today*, and Frau Schneider gave Terri permission for us to use the symbol on a variety of new products, such as the T-shirts and costume jewelry you see around our store."

"Have you or Terri ever actually *seen* these artifacts or do you know anything about their history?" I went on, my curiosity now fully piqued.

"No," Eric replied. "Frankly, I've never really given it much thought. I'll tell you what though; I can give you Ludwig's phone number if you would like to follow this up."

The following excerpt is taken from the Preface of our book, *The Messianic Seal of the Jerusalem Church*, © 1999 by Olim Publications, Tiberias, Israel.

> On Friday, February 5, 1999, we (Rueven Schmalz and myself) were ushered by a uniformed maid into Ludwig Schneider's voluminous library in the Schneider residence in Jerusalem.
>
> Ludwig Schneider is a man with a powerful, classic German face, a bright smile, and piercing, sky-blue eyes. His obvious vitality and almost

boyish manner seem somehow to conflict with his easy flowing, Germanesque formality, belying his fifty-eight years.

Within moments we were holding the first of the eight awesome relics in our hands— a brick-sized rectangle of local marble, adorned with an etched version of the ancient symbol, and words in archaic Aramaic letters proclaiming: "For the oil of the Spirit." An interesting difference in this piece from the others: a tiny etched cross formed the fish's eye.

One of the other remarkable pieces was a small ceramic vial, appearing like it could well have been used to hold anointing oil, and originally have been placed upon the "stand for anointing oil." Both of these, like all of the artifacts, were found in the same place, in a grotto adjacent to the upper room, which is located directly astride the ancient and revered tomb of King David.

Another piece is the remains of a small marble pillar, and the others, an assortment of various-sized pottery shards with painted versions of the symbol. All of these artifacts are etched, embossed or painted with renditions of the same three-part symbol of menorah, star of David and fish.

All of the pieces were unquestionably authentic to even an amateur eye. To Reuven, a self-trained historian and archeologist, sculptor, and long-time student of the early Church and first century history in general, these pieces were clearly genuine.

Finally, after we both, with awe, had carefully examined each of the eight pieces, Ludwig's wife served us Turkish coffee, which we sipped as Ludwig told his tantalizing story·

"In 1990," Ludwig began in good English, flavored with a delightful old world sounding German accent, "I became acquainted with Tech Oteeoos, a Greek Orthodox monk in his nineties who lived by himself in an obscure, dank and foul smelling, small building in the Old City of Jerusalem. I was drawn to the ancient monk whom I visited several times. I kept my distance until he could emerge into the fresh air. The human stench of the dwelling kept me from exploring its interior.

"One day," Ludwig continued, "I believe it was on my third visit, Tech Oteeoos showed me, to my absolute amazement, several ancient artifacts which he had excavated at a site on Mount Zion, in the vicinity of the building traditionally known as the original Church founded by James the Just, the brother of Jesus. The central feature of each piece was a hand-executed rendition of the symbol, either etched into or painted upon the surface of the stone.

"Needless to say, I was fascinated by both the symbol and its obvious significance. It was clear to me that God Himself had laid before me a long-forgotten testimony informing the world about the true roots of the Church.

"Several visits later, the old monk finally lured me into the interior of his foul-smelling dwelling. It was there that I saw, for the first time, his collection of about thirty to forty beautiful and varied pieces, all bearing the three-part symbol. As I stared at this treasure in wonder, my host carefully selected eight of the pieces which he later, during a subsequent visit, presented to me as a gift. On this occasion, I excitedly photographed the eight artifacts which had been set aside for me.

"But an even greater gift from this dear messenger of God lay in store for me. During a subsequent visit, after he had, as usual, devoured my chocolate bar gift, he took me by the hand and led me to the nearby site where he had personally excavated his entire collection. This special place was an obviously very old Jewish *mikva* located near the Tomb of David.

"After we had climbed over an unimposing fence, the old man led me down the traditional seven cosmic stairs leading to the place used for ceremonial cleansing. We proceeded past this place, and entered a catacomb that continued on into the quickly fading light. After what seemed like a short distance, just before the first bend, my ancient monk friend and benefactor was excitedly pointing out his special gift to me on one of the walls, a perfect rendition of the three-part symbol etched into the stone.

"In my initial excitement, I went rushing back to the priests of the monastery to report this incredible find. I was shocked by the audience I received. They rebuffed me, refused to answer my questions about the "Seal" and locked me outside of the monastery gate.

"I was overwhelmed by the great significance of the find and its meaning to the Church and the entire world," Ludwig continued, "and I determined with confidence, that I should bring these artifacts to the attention of the Israel Museum so they, in turn, could promulgate their incredible message to the world. Thus I called the curator of the museum and made an appointment.

"The curator was most friendly, even gracious. I was ushered into his office with the pictures of the eight pieces which he examined with careful and studied interest. He then told me matter-of-factly that the museum already had other artifacts with this very same three-part symbol that had come to them from other sources which he did not specify. The curator assured me that the museum had firm plans to have a special exhibition of these artifacts and their unique symbol, and that they would make an announcement regarding them to the world press in the near future. This was in 1990. Quite frankly, I am not surprised that these artifacts or the three-part symbol with which they are adorned have as yet, as far as I know, never emerged, nor has any information about them. Israeli officialdom, perhaps, was afraid of what the world might think if the truth became known: the early Church was Jewish, and the original believers in Jesus were Jews.

"You can't imagine my frustration over this seeming suppression, but even more, my sorrow when I returned for a somewhat delayed visit to my dear benefactor Tech Oteeoos. Tearfully, I

learned that he had died, and irrespective of his
earlier promise that the rest of the pieces were to
be mine, his dwelling had been completely emp-
tied, and all of his remaining treasure had vanished.

"Despite the passage of years, I couldn't stop
thinking about the importance of the symbol and
the need to present it to the world. It was thus in
1996 that I opened a small gift shop in the Old
City where I sold traditional tourist gift items, to
which I added several products bearing a simple
artist's rendition of the ancient symbol.

"Within days, I was threatened by Orthodox
rabbis who insisted that I remove these 'evil, hea-
then' objects from my shop. By now, although
none had any idea about the profound significance of their purchases, tourists had begun to
enthusiastically buy my symbol adorned sou-
venirs in sufficient quantity to entice my nearby
competitor shops (some owned by Orthodox
Jews) to produce and offer for sale, copies of my
unique products.

"This unfriendly competition wasn't to last
long. When I refused to remove these items from
my shop, the Orthodox gathered outside in large
numbers and stoned the place, breaking my windows: not once, but several times. I finally gave
up and closed my shop less than a year after it
had been opened, taking little satisfaction from
the fact that the other shops had also soon
removed the symbol-carrying products from their
own shelves. Presumably, between the combined
efforts of the Israel Museum and the Orthodox

rabbis, the precious symbol proclaiming the true origins of the Church had vanished from public view.

"My earnest prayer," Ludwig concluded, "is that the truth about the Jewish origins of the Christian Church will be made known throughout the world so that all might know: Jesus was a Jew, the early (first century) Church in Jerusalem was attended exclusively by a sect of Essene Jews who had accepted Jesus as their Messiah, and the entire Church in the world today has been built upon this precious Jewish foundation."

The idea to write a book about this monumentally important symbol at first took the form of what was to be an historical essay written by Reuven and published by Olim Creative Products. This original approach quickly evolved from a simple essay into a two-part book: Part One, to be written by Reuven, from an historical perspective dealing with the time leading up to the First Nazarene Synagogue on Mount Zion as well as the early history of the Nazarene movement; I, in turn, was to write Part Two, a biblical interpretation of  the meaning and message of the symbol.

The Schneider family took several weeks of deliberations to determine if they should proceed with a formal business arrangement between them and Olim Creative Products, where we would have their permission and full cooperation in writing our book and the opportunity to take photographs and "strikes" (using an alginate dental impression material) from the two artifacts upon which the symbol had been etched (as opposed to painted). In turn, we were to pay the Schneiders a royalty on all gross sales of the book and any other products derived from the photographs and the "strikes."

The three of us, Donna, Reuven and myself, were engrossed in excited conversation as we neared Tiberias on our trip home from Jerusalem. Reuven and I had again visited the Schneiders, and Donna had come along with us to see the artifacts for herself. After we had finalized the business agreement, we immediately took the promised photographs and "strikes." Now, on the way home, we spoke of nothing else.

"Reuven, has it dawned on you that we don't have a name for the symbol?" I ventured. "We obviously *need* one."

"What would you think of 'the Messianic Seal of James the Just?'" Reuven immediately offered.

"Hmmm," I replied after a few moments of consideration. "Sounds good, but a bit too specific. How about 'The Messianic Seal of the Jerusalem Church'?"

We introduced our book by this same title at the Christian Booksellers Convention in Orlando, Florida in July 1999. Considering that we started with virtually no distribution arrangements, the book was an instant success. The first printing sold out by November, and the second by the middle of 2000. Now, a year later, we are entering into the fourth edition and we have only just begun to establish viable worldwide distribution.

International attention took a specific form at the Feast of Tabernacles celebration in Jerusalem in October 1999 when a French publisher took great interest in the book. Just recently, we have received the first authors' copies of the resulting French edition.

The Lord was again quite specific when, shortly after we had introduced our first book, He led me, to begin writing *The Children of God*. This second, much longer work (310 pages) was published in July 2000 and was formally introduced two months later at the Feast of Tabernacles celebration in Jerusalem. The book focuses on several overlapping themes, all of which in one way or another relate to the Jewish roots of the Christian Church. It was an immediate success, and now, less than a year after it was introduced, we are about to enter into our third printing. Barbara Richmond, Director of For Your Glory Ministries was kind enough to write the foreword. She has called this work "the textbook for the Return to the Jewish Roots Movement." She went on to comment:

> *The Children of God* is an absolute masterpiece!!!!! Bob Fischer has made a contribution of immense value and significance to the Jewish Roots Movement. We must applaud his extensive research and insightful analysis which has produced a foundational classic for all who seek to be a part of this move of the Spirit in our day.

Sid Roth, Director of Messianic Vision Ministries was also very kind in his evaluation. He devoted his entire January 2001 News Letter to the work. He concluded his comments with:

> There are many books about the history of the first Church, but *The Children of God* by Bob Fischer is the best one I have seen yet. With all I have read on the subject, I was still shocked at how many pagan practices are found in both Protestantism and Catholicism. Every Christian in America must read this thorough, yet easily understood book.

Then, even before I finished the first draft of this second book, the Lord once again called me to write *Provision*, the book that you now hold in your hand. And, as if this weren't enough, He has clearly shown me that there are to be at least two more works to follow. Even now, as I make my final review of this manuscript , I marvel at the fact that the Lord has already deeply immersed me in  writing my next book.

## Chapter Seven

## Prophecy Fulfilled: The Beginning of Another Rainbow

*And so we have the prophetic word confirmed, which you do well to heed as a light that shines in a dark place, until the day dawns and the morning star rises in your hearts;* (2 Pet 1:19)

Quite late one evening last winter, when I was struggling with a seasonal upper respiratory viral attack,  Eric Morey called me from The Galilee Experience to deliver an  uncharacteristically, for him, insistent message. "Bob, you've just *got* to come down here and meet Pastor Bob Johnson. He's here with a group of people from Kansas City and he *won't* take no for an answer!"

"Really, Eric," I tried to extricate myself from the grips of this impending commitment, "I feel *terrible!* Who is this guy, anyway?"

"He's one of your biggest fans who is,  as we speak, buying all of your books he and his people can carry—he's also the pastor of one of the biggest and most influential Assembly of God

Churches in the Midwest!"

"Okay," I relented, a decision that has turned out to be one of the wisest I've ever made.

Pastor Bob Johnson and I instantly "connected." I knew from the moment I shook the hand of this beautiful brother that our meeting was a divine appointment.

Eric, who had introduced me to Bob Johnson, left me at a table in The Galilee Experience Cafe with  Bob, his lovely wife Sonja, and Darrell Jones, pastor of Grace Evangelical Church in St. Joseph, Missouri. Both pastors didn't take long in getting to the *real* purpose of our meeting.

After making some very strong supportive comments about how important they felt my two books were to their ministries and to the Church at large, Bob asked me forthrightly: "What would it take to get you to come to Kansas City on a speaking tour?"

I heard myself answering without a moment's hesitation. "Nothing more than a round trip airplane ticket."

He continued. "When would it be most convenient for you to come, say, arriving on a Saturday and departing a week from the following Monday?"

Again I responded right off the top of my head. "Any time this spring would work fine for me—ideally, I'd choose the first week in May."

"Let's plan on it!" Bob said with finality, closing the deal which had taken less than two minutes to present, discuss and consummate.

My heart was racing with excitement. "Just what do you have planned for the week," I ventured after catching my breath.

"Darrell and I work with about twelve local area churches. What we figure is that you will spend your first Sunday at Darrell's church in St. Joe, then  the rest of the week, speaking each evening in other area Churches,  finally ending up with me at Grandview Assembly on your second Sunday. Don't worry, Bob," he smiled knowingly. "We will keep you very busy indeed. You will be very greatly blessed."

"I already *have been* greatly blessed," I assured my two new pastor friends. "I'm thrilled and honored by your invitation!"

When the Lord engineers something, I never cease to be amazed at how He keeps adding blessing upon blessing. Within days of my meeting with these two precious pastors, Donna and I got a call from Don and Karolyn Killian and their companion, David Simpson. It seems these three believers were with a tour group in the area and, having heard we attended Carmel Assembly, in Haifa, on Mt Carmel, were wondering if we might be able to give them a ride to our fellowship on the upcoming Shabbat. We immediately agreed with delight to do so.

Meeting these three lovely people was another divine appointment to the same purpose. I found myself not being surprised to learn that they were in the leadership of Harvest House, a ministry in Destin, Florida, the very same place of so many of Donna's and my most treasured memories. Nor was I surprised when they asked me almost immediately after we met "what it would take" for me to present a seminar on the Jewish roots of the Church to their group. Before the day ended, we had made a tentative date that dovetailed perfectly with my Kansas City schedule.

But there was even to be more. A few days later, I was speaking with Barbara Richmond by phone about another totally unrelated matter. During the course of the conversation, I just happened to bring up my invitation to speak at Grandview Assembly since I knew that Barbara had already spoken there, and I hoped to get some sense of what to expect.

"How wonderful, Bob!" she responded  excitedly. "Since you are going to be in the States through May, 'what would it take' to get you to speak at the Tenth Anniversary Convention of my ministry, For Your Glory? It will be in Colorado Springs May 31 through June 2."

Needless to say, the dates worked perfectly, and I felt more than just a little honored and thrilled to accept yet another wonderful invitation.

What with all of this amazing movement, I found myself once again caught up in the pitfall of, strictly on my own, trying to make something wonderful from the Lord even better. After all, I reasoned, if I was to be speaking in the Kansas City area, why not expand this to nearby Tulsa, the home of some of our company's original and still strongest supporters. Thus I suggested to my Tulsa friends, that they set up a series of engagements for me during the week following my schedule in Kansas City. It was really awesome how the Lord made it clear that we were going to do this speaking tour entirely *His* way and not partly mine. Tentative arrangement followed tentative arrangement and each in turn, for a variety of reasons, did not materialize. Finally, I began to catch on that this was the Lord's schedule, not mine, and I stopped trying to make something happen that was obviously not in His plan.

I would never deny nor would my wife argue against the idea that Mother Fischer raised at least one absolutely determined boy! I had "made up my head" that, come what may, I was going to finish the first draft of *Provision* before my upcoming speaking tour to the States. I was really *into* this book, on a roll, and had practically chained myself to my computer in a whirlwind effort to finish this work. By finishing the first draft, I reasoned, Nirit Zagofsky, my editor, who was already working on Part One, would have these several weeks while I was out of the country to fine-tune the rest of the manuscript so as to allow its accelerated publication, which, I reasoned, could occur even as early as late summer.

On the first of March, I handed the finished draft of Part Two to Donna for her usual first screening and suggestions. I was quite taken aback by her comment as I did so.

"Are you ready for your upcoming speaking tour?" she asked matter of factly.

I found myself on the defensive. "No, I am not," I replied, anticipating her next comment.

"Then don't you think you should get started? You leave for Kansas City in two months, and if I know you, you will want to spend a lot of time on this."

I couldn't argue with her very poignant observation. She was absolutely right. Like it or not, I had to shift gears and delay my writing until later. The task was anything but unpleasant, and I soon found myself deeply immersed in drafting a series of over-head projector transparencies that tracked the central themes in my two books, along with some new, related material that had recently come to my attention.

Even though I was thoroughly involved in this new project that in the end produced sixty-five visual aids, as I proceeded, I nevertheless found myself fretting from time to time that I had found it necessary, as a matter of priority, to abandon completing my latest book. The Lord, in His infinite mercy, put my fretting to a sudden halt one day when I was in the midst of my not infrequent lamenting. He told me in His special unmistakable way: "Never mind about not completing the book right now. I planned it this way. I have *more* for you in Kansas City."

I didn't have a clue what He might be talking about, but I trusted the fact that it was He who had conveyed this very clear instruction, and so I found myself much more able to complete preparations for my upcoming trip without further hesitation or complaint.

As I became totally absorbed in preparing the visual aids, I found myself frequently marveling at how the Lord was fulfilling the prophecy given through Gene Bacon that I would be taking the word from Zion to the nations.

The Lord God of Israel, however, never does anything halfway. He is entirely faithful to His word. Since my quickly evolving writing and speaking outreach to the nations was only one side of the promise, I was thrilled and delighted, but not surprised when I got a series of related and excited e-mails from Marty and Rob outlining some genuinely amazing personnel, material, financial and other assorted happenings within Olim North America. It seems, they explained, the *Awakening* line had suddenly awoken! A ready and able customer had just placed a large order that would be shipped to the States the very week I would begin my speaking tour in Kansas City.

A short time before I departed for Kansas City, the Lord blessed me greatly with not one but two genuinely remarkable signs and wonders. The first occurred while I was walking a few blocks to my parked car from our clinic, where I had gone to pick up a supply of my medications to tide me over for the several weeks that I would be out of the country.

Since I have a well-founded fear of snakes, I would normally never even have thought of taking a shortcut across the diagonal of a former gravel parking lot which was now overgrown with an almost complete covering of waist-high, thick weeds. I knew that deadly vipers lurked in these kinds of places, and it thus made every bit of good sense to walk the relatively short extra distance around this threatening obstacle.Even so, without any conscious thought whatsoever, I found myself cutting across the foreboding diagonal, wandering at random through a sort of maze of several natural, very narrow and short, sometimes connecting pathways through the thick green growth. As I did so, I found myself praying, not only for protection, but also in a rising sense of thanksgiving—something yet unknown, something wonderful was about to occur.

Then it happened! As I approached a small weed-free clearing, I was almost blinded by the glaring brightness of the sun reflecting directly into my eyes from a nearby point on the ground in front of me. It was an astounding, breathtaking vision of divine, gleaming gold! I could hardly remain standing in the presence of such glorious wonderment. Slowly, reverently, I approached the source of this amazingly bright, golden, reflected light. Then, as I bent down for a closer look, I beheld an incredibly perfect, "mint proof" ten agorote coin, the equivalent of an American dime. I noted that the absolutely flawless brass coin with a menorah stamped on its face, was propped against a small stone in such a manner that it was aligned to reflect the sun directly in my face as I had approached.

This marvelous coin has now joined my collection of the very special, God-provided coin signs I have accumulated since I found the very first of them on the threshold of my Boeing office. Just how long it had been waiting for me in this potentially dangerous place I cannot say, but I know with certainty that it was placed there for me by the very hand of God as an unmistakable confirmation—what I was now doing with my life was, at least for this moment, right in the center of His will.

Soon after we introduced *The Messianic Seal of the Jerusalem Church*, Reuven had begun to frequently declare his intense desire to write a much longer, scholarly follow-up to what he had already written in Part One of our book. Since Reuven, at the time of this first writing, was neither "computer literate" nor knew how to type, I had laboriously undertaken the onerous task of transcribing his barely legible, all upper case handwritten scrawl into a typed manuscript. Thus, while I supported and encouraged him to write this next book, at the same time I proclaimed that never again would I attempt to help him in the same secretarial way as I had with his earlier efforts. Where his determination and my rebellion led was to a contract between us where we agreed I would supply him with a computer which he would first use to learn how to type. Then, he committed to submit, within one year, on a first-right-of-refusal basis, the completed manuscript of his new book to Olim Publications, a new working entity of Olim Creative Products. Since we had finalized these arrangements not long before my departure for the States, the same day I was to pack for the trip, I found myself driving along the shore of the Sea of Galilee en route to Reuven's nearby settlement house with a final bit of software I had purchased for his new computer.

It was a lovely day. There had just been a hint of badly needed rain. Now the sun had fully returned and was reflecting radiantly from the surface of the water upon which, I reverently contemplated, Yeshua had once walked, perhaps in the very place where I now found myself glancing as I drove along the somewhat twisty, narrow, two-lane road.

Then I saw it! Before my eyes God had placed yet another phenomenal sign. There, seemingly no more than fifty meters from the place where I sat, I beheld the originating end, the very literal beginning of the most perfectly beautiful rainbow I have ever seen. It seemed close enough to touch, and it stretched from its origin at my fingertips in a perfect arc leading to the Golan Heights on the opposite shore.

I am at a loss for words to properly describe the majesty, the absolute perfection, the spiritual wonderment and incredible beauty of this, yet another confirming sign—the Lord God of Israel was already blessing what lay ahead for me in the coming days.

Two months before my departure, I had shipped by surface a

cubic meter of my books (about 1,000 of each) to myself in care of Pastor Bob Johnson at Grandview Assembly. I had been assured by my shipping agent that this was plenty of time for them to arrive and be waiting for me. My plan was to have a good supply available to offer for sale at my various upcoming speaking engagements. Bob Johnson had promised to e-mail me when the shipment arrived, and when I did not hear from him before I left Israel, I found myself praying that this had only been an oversight on his part and that the books, by now, had arrived in good order. After all, Donna and I, our prayer group, and others had all been praying that these books would arrive in Kansas City before I did, so "what to worry?" I kept reassuring myself.

It was thus, when I saw Bob Johnson's sweet smile of welcoming at Kansas City International Airport, it didn't take long for me to inquire, "So what's the deal on my books?"

Bob gave me his long-practiced and well-perfected pastoral comforting look. "The good news is," he began, "the shipment made it just fine to the United States. The bad news is that your pallet just happened to be placed in a container with some farm equipment transshipped from Europe. Consequently, it seems that the Department of Agricultural impounded the whole container because of the hoof and mouth disease scare."

"Oh, no!" I exclaimed. "Did they give you any idea when the books will be released?"

One has to really get to know Bob Johnson to fully appreciate both the depth of his love for people and his compelling sense of humor. "That's more of the good news," he added in his impish way with wonderful timing. "I worked with the shipping people all morning, and the pallet was delivered to the Church about twenty minutes before I had to leave to pick you up here at the airport. Isn't the Lord good?"

"Indeed He is!" I readily agreed.

After a short and almost sleepless night, nearly overcome by jet lag, some twelve hours after my arrival in the States, I found myself praying for God's favor as I was graciously being introduced by Pastor Darrell Jones to several hundred members of his congregation who were attending the first of two morning services. As I entered the pulpit, I felt more like an observer than a participant. Strangely, yet still joyfully, I found myself in a bizarre, out-of-body, unexplainable way, "listening" rather than speaking. I *knew* in my spirit, that the Holy Spirit had taken over, and I marveled at what was happening.

As the first service ended, I quietly and thankfully anticipated a nearly two-hour respite, along with several cups of coffee that would bolster me for the upcoming second service. But this was not to be.

"It's time for adult Sunday School," Darrell announced, reminding me of my earlier commitment to teach this class between services. "We are really looking forward to your teaching on the pagan roots of the Church. This fits in perfectly to what I have been presenting over the past couple of months."

The class, consisting of virtually the entire congregation, had been wonderfully attentive and responsive, and in the end, I did have time for a quick cup of coffee before the second morning service. But, by now, I didn't really need coffee. Never mind the lack of sleep, jet lag and the heavy schedule—I was *alive* in my spirit! Never before in my life had I experienced such a sense of sheer *fulfillment*! I knew that I knew—I was doing *precisely* what the Lord had planned for this very moment of my life.

One wonderful and gloriously fulfilling experience followed the next, as I accomplished the very full schedule Bob Johnson had prepared for my several days in the Kansas City area. I can't say to what extent my presence with these several thousands of beautiful believers in Yeshua may have blessed them. I can say, however, with absolute certainly how very greatly they all blessed me.

One of the many highlights of these speaking engagements occurred on my last day in Colorado Springs when, from the pulpit of Day Spring Assembly, I looked out over the large congregation and beheld the lovely faces of my very dear and old friends, Sheryl and Daniel Joseph, who had come down from Denver where they now lived, to meet with me in a blessed reunion. I must confess that when I introduced them to the congregation it was very difficult for me to choke back my tears of joy. I might also say that I wasn't one bit surprised by the fact that immediately after my message, Daniel rushed up to the pulpit to report to me the details of yet another vision he had just received for me. Should it be fulfilled, and I have no reason to expect otherwise, it will no doubt be the subject of yet another book.

Perhaps the best way for me to summarize my incredible blessings from my time in Kansas City, and those equally wonderful following times in Destin, Florida and Colorado Springs is to share what happened on my second Sunday, at the end of the first morning service at Grandview Assembly.

As I concluded my teaching, Pastor Johnson  invited those from the congregation who felt so led to come forward to the altar to be anointed with oil by "this spirit filled brother from Israel."

I was totally surprised by this invitation and considered it a great privilege to have an opportunity to minister in this way to what I imagined would be a typical few who might respond.

Instead, however, the entire congregation of several hundred immediately formed a seemingly unending line in response to their pastor's call. It was my great honor and privilege to minister to them all, anointing and praying for each: entire families, individuals, young and old, most of them in tears, barely visible to me through the continuing flood of my own. This special time of ministry continued on into the time for the next service. Then, at the end of this second gathering, the same invitation was given with the same response. The anointing and individual prayer continued into the early afternoon. Then, that evening, at a service in Clinton, Missouri, Pastor Jerry Baughman gave the same invitation which evoked the same response.

Praise the Lord God of Israel for He has been my perfect and full provision for all of the years of my already long life. Now, having just returned to Tiberias, I once again find myself totally immersed in finishing *Provision*. As I conclude this book, in which I have recounted but only a few from the myriad of signs, wonders and miracles with which the Lord has so graciously seasoned my way, I can't stop the flood of excited anticipation as I remember the most recent rainbow He set before me as I drove toward Reuven's home along the shore of the Sea of Galilee. Now, in my spirit, I return to that glorious, clearly defined, remarkable and holy place on the water: the very place where this rainbow began.

"Yes, O Lord God of Israel," I cry out with all my being. "Joyfully and with profound thanksgiving, I take Your hand as You guide me along this vibrantly beautiful bow, partaking of whatever other wonderful blessings You may have for me along the way, until at last, safe and secure in Your love, I arrive on the other even more glorious and resplendent distant shore.

## After Word

*These all wait for You, that You may give them their food in due season. What You give them they gather in; you open Your hand, they are filled with good. You hide Your face, they are troubled; you take away their breath, they die and return to their dust. You send forth Your Spirit, they are created; and You renew the face of the earth. (Ps 104:27-30)*

*And I will pray the Father, and He will give you another Helper, that He may abide with you for-ever—the Spirit of truth, whom the world cannot receive, because it neither sees Him nor knows Him; but you know Him, for He dwells with you and will be in you. I will not leave you orphans; I will come to you. A little while longer and the world will see Me no more, but you will see Me. Because I live, you will live also. At that day you will know that I am in My Father, and you in Me, and I in you. (John 14:16-20)*

The Lord God of Israel, YHWH (*I Was, I Am, I Will Be*) is His Name. He has provided the heavens and the earth and all that dwells therein. He has wondrously created you and created me as a provision for Himself so that we might worship Him in spirit and in truth, bringing glory unto glory. He provides each of our life-sustaining breaths—not one is taken in or given out without His specific direction. He is the author of our every heartbeat. He numbered them all before the beginning of time. Each of the uncountable myriad of minuscule components with which He has constructed our physical beings are utterly dependent upon Him for their continuance.

Holy, holy, holy is the Lord of hosts; the whole earth is full of His glory! Who was and is and is to come, Creator of heaven and earth. He is the provider of everything!

During the nearly four centuries when Solomon's Temple stood on Mount Moriah, once each year, only on Yom Kippur, the sacred day of atonement, the high priest entered through double doors made of olive wood into the holy of holies, a 20-cubit (30-foot) cube. In that room, two cherubim, each ten feet tall, stood with outstretched wings. Two of the wings met above the ark of the covenant, and two of them touched the north and south walls of the room. The Lord God of Israel's presence was manifested in this holiest of all places as a radiant cloud.

The ark of the covenant was designed by YHWH to provide a meeting place, the most sacred of all places, for Himself and the high priest, where He would dispense His great mercy to His people after their atonement.

> *And there I will meet with you, and I will speak with you from above the mercy seat, from between the two cherubim which are on the ark of the Testimony, about everything which I will*

*give you in commandment to the children of
Israel.* (Exod 25:22)

Before entering the holy of holies on this special day, the high
priest sacrificed a bull for himself and his house. After properly
preparing himself, according to Scripture, he then entered this
holiest of all places, the throne room. Upon entering, he first
burned incense so that clouds of sweet odors at once arose and
practically hid the *Shekhinah* of God radiating from the golden
mercy seat covering of the ark of the covenant.

Had the high priest not done this, he would not have dared to
look upon this essence of the divine presence.

Having made all ordained preparation, the high priest then,
using one of his fingers, seven times sprinkled blood from the
previously slain bull upon the mercy seat. This blood was thus
sprinkled to acknowledge that, because of their sins of the past
year, he and his house were unclean and deserved death but
because of this blood, they had cried out for and then received
forgiveness and cleansing. For the high priest, his house, and the
people, atonement had now been made—all had been cleansed
with blood.

The prophet Jeremiah began his ministry in 627 BCE and it
continued for the next forty years, until Solomon's Temple was
destroyed in 587 BCE. At some point during this time, he prophesied:

> *"Then it shall come to pass, when you are multi-
> plied and increased in the land in those days,"
> says the LORD, "that they will say no more, 'The
> ark of the covenant of the LORD.' It shall not
> come to mind, nor shall they remember it, nor
> shall they visit it, nor shall it be made anymore.*

*"At that time Jerusalem shall be called The
Throne of the LORD, and all the nations shall be
gathered to it, to the name of the LORD, to
Jerusalem. No more shall they follow the dictates
of their evil hearts.* (Jer 3:16-17)

*"Behold, the days are coming, says the LORD,
when I will make a new covenant with the house
of Israel and with the house of Judah—* *"not
according to the covenant that I made with their
fathers in the day that I took them by the hand to
lead them out of the land of Egypt, My covenant
which they broke, though I was a husband to
them, says the LORD. "But this is the covenant
that I will make with the house of Israel after
those days, says the LORD: I will put My law in
their minds, and write it on their hearts; and I
will be their God, and they shall be My people.*
(Jer 31:31-33)

The Lord God of Israel thus spoke through His prophet
Jeremiah to His people. The sacrificial system set forth in the old
covenant would be superseded by the shed blood of Yeshua, the
soon coming Messiah of the new covenant. Thus, the ark of the
covenant would not only no longer be needed--it would, ultimately,  be forgotten and never again seen on this earth.

*But Christ came as High Priest of the good things
to come, with the greater and more perfect taber-
nacle not made with hands, that is, not of this
creation. Not with the blood of goats and calves,*

*but with His own blood He entered the Most Holy
Place once for all, having obtained eternal
redemption.* (Heb 9:11-12)

The prophet Isaiah, writing more than a century before
Jeremiah, described, in some detail the coming Messiah, Yeshua,
who would fulfill this new covenant:

*Who has believed our report? And to whom has
the arm of the LORD been revealed? For He shall
grow up before Him as a tender plant, and as a
root out of dry ground. He has no form or come-
liness; and when we see Him, there is no beauty
that we should desire Him. He is despised and
rejected by men, a Man of sorrows and acquainted with grief. And we hid, as it were, our faces
from Him; he was despised, and we did not
esteem Him. Surely He has borne our griefs and
carried our sorrows; yet we esteemed Him strick-
en, smitten by God, and afflicted. But He was
wounded for our transgressions, he was bruised
for our iniquities; the chastisement for our peace
was upon Him, and by His stripes we are healed.
All we like sheep have gone astray; we have
turned, every one, to his own way; and the LORD
has laid on Him the iniquity of us all. He was
oppressed and He was afflicted, yet He opened
not His mouth; he was led as a lamb to the
slaughter, and as a sheep before its shearers is
silent, so He opened not His mouth. He was taken
from prison and from judgment, and who will*

*declare His generation? For He was cut off from the land of the living; for the transgressions of My people He was stricken. And they made His grave with the wicked— but with the rich at His death, because He had done no violence, nor was any deceit in His mouth. Yet it pleased the LORD to bruise Him; he has put Him to grief. When You make His soul an offering for sin, he shall see His seed, He shall prolong His days, and the pleasure of the LORD shall prosper in His hand. He shall see the labor of His soul, and be satisfied. By His knowledge My righteous Servant shall justify many, for He shall bear their iniquities. Therefore I will divide Him a portion with the great, and He shall divide the spoil with the strong, because He poured out His soul unto death, and He was numbered with the transgressors, and He bore the sin of many, and made intercession for the transgressors.* (Isa 53:1-12)

Profoundly, and even more specifically, King David, sometime during his forty year reign, even before his son Solomon built the first temple, described the coming Messiah and His fate in terrible and exquisite detail:

*My God, My God, why have You forsaken Me? Why are You so far from helping Me, and from the words of My groaning? O My God, I cry in the daytime, but You do not hear; and in the night season, and am not silent. But You are holy, enthroned in the praises of Israel. Our fathers*

*trusted in You; they trusted, and You delivered
them. They cried to You, and were delivered; they
trusted in You, and were not ashamed. But I am
a worm, and no man; a reproach of men, and
despised of the people. All those who see Me
ridicule Me; they shoot out the lip, they shake the
head, saying, "He trusted in the LORD, let Him
rescue Him; let Him deliver Him, since He
delights in Him!" But You are He who took Me
out of the womb; you made Me trust while on My
mother's breasts. I was cast upon You from birth.
From My mother's womb you have been My God.
Be not far from Me, for trouble is near; for there
is none to help. Many bulls have surrounded Me;
strong bulls of Bashan have encircled Me. They
gape at Me with their mouths, like a raging and
roaring lion. I am poured out like water, and all
My bones are out of joint; my heart is like wax; it
has melted within Me. My strength is dried up like
a potsherd, and My tongue clings to My jaws; you
have brought Me to the dust of death. For dogs
have surrounded Me; the congregation of the
wicked has enclosed Me. They pierced My hands
and My feet; I can count all My bones. They look
and stare at Me. They divide My garments among
them, and for My clothing they cast lots. But You,
O LORD, do not be far from Me; O My Strength,
hasten to help Me! Deliver Me from the sword, my
precious life from the power of the dog. Save Me
from the lion's mouth and from the horns of the
wild oxen! You have answered Me. I will declare
Your name to My brethren; in the midst of the
assembly I will praise You. You who fear the*

*LORD, praise Him! All you descendants of Jacob, glorify Him, and fear Him, all you offspring of Israel! For He has not despised nor abhorred the affliction of the afflicted; nor has He hidden His face from Him; but when He cried to Him, He heard. My praise shall be of You in the great assembly; I will pay My vows before those who fear Him. The poor shall eat and be satisfied; those who seek Him will praise the LORD. Let your heart live forever! All the ends of the world shall remember and turn to the LORD, and all the families of the nations shall worship before You. For the kingdom is the LORD'S, and He rules over the nations. All the prosperous of the earth shall eat and worship; all those who go down to the dust shall bow before Him, even he who cannot keep himself alive. A posterity shall serve Him. It will be recounted of the Lord to the next generation, They will come and declare His righteousness to a people who will be born, that He has done this.* (Ps 22:1-31)

Just as Jeremiah prophesied, after the temple of Solomon had been destroyed, the ark of the covenant and the *Shekhinah* of God were absent from the two temples that followed in its place. As the people hungered and continued to cry out for their God— finally, some six hundred years later, He appeared, as prophesied, born of a virgin in Bethlehem in the most humble of circumstances.

Yeshua boldly proclaimed His divinity—that He was the one who had been promised, and the absolute need for those who heard this good news to embrace Him.

*Jesus said to him, "I am the way, the truth, and the life. No one comes to the Father except through Me.* (John 14:6)

Then, on the night He was betrayed, as Yeshua conducted a *Pesach seder* for His disciples in the Upper Room on Mount Zion, He taught us all concerning the amazing power and meaning of His precious body that was about to be given and His precious blood that was about to be shed the next day for the forgiveness of all our sins, *once and for all.*

*And as they were eating, Jesus took bread, blessed and broke it, and gave it to the disciples and said, "Take, eat; this is My body." Then He took the cup, and gave thanks, and gave it to them, saying, "Drink from it, all of you. "For this is My blood of the new covenant, which is shed for many for the remission of sins. "But I say to you, I will not drink of this fruit of the vine from now on until that day when I drink it new with you in My Father's kingdom."* (Matt 26:27-29)

The day after the *Pesach seder* when He was crucified in a place called Golgotha, a Roman soldier plunged a spear into Yeshua's side, probably penetrating both his spleen and his heart. The event was recorded as a testimony by the disciple whom He loved:

*But when they came to Jesus and saw that He was already dead, they did not break His legs. But one of the soldiers pierced His side with a spear, and immediately blood and water came out. And he who has seen has testified, and his testimony is true; and he knows that he is telling the truth, so that you may believe.* (John 19:33-35)

In recent years, there has been a remarkable and, understandably, highly controversial claim:

Just before the first temple was destroyed, the ark of the covenant was hidden by Jeremiah in a cavern twenty feet directly below the place where Yeshua was to be crucified some six hundred years later. Next, the claim continues, at the moment Yeshua died, there was an earthquake, referred to in Scripture, that caused a deep crack in the rock extending from the foot of Yeshua's cross all the way down to and including the cover of a stone case that held the ark of the covenant, therefore exposing the mercy seat.

Then, this amazing claim continues, the blood ran out from Yeshua's side, down through the crack in the rock until it finally splashed upon the mercy seat. It is further claimed, with a great deal of detail and documentation (the validity and sufficiency of which is at the center of the controversy), that the ark of the covenant has been found at this very same location in Jerusalem, near the Garden Tomb and a place that is still called Golgotha. Further, the claim continues, samples of the blood have been taken and an analysis of this blood shows it to have come from a male who was the product of a virgin birth, in that it contains only half of the number of chromosome pairs found in normal two-human-parent beings.

I first heard the essence of this amazing story from Pastor Bob Johnson during my recent speaking tour in Kansas City. He offered it only for my consideration, sharing with me no position as to his personal sense of its truth or lack thereof. I have since interviewed two eye witnesses, viewed several videos and read several books and articles related to this claim. Quite frankly, after all this, I am not fully convinced, one way or the other, as to its truthfulness.

All the while I have been investigating this matter, I have been seeking the Lord: Was this the "Something *more* I have for you in Kansas City" He told me about as I left this present writing for a time to prepare for my recently completed speaking tour? Or was the "something else" perhaps some of the other wonderful happenings I have earlier shared, such as the one-hundred-percent altar calls where entire congregations came forward to be anointed with oil from Israel?

Now, as I conclude these pages, I believe that the Lord, the Great Provider of everything, has, in His mercy and grace,  provided an answer to my enigma:

While it is certainly very important and of great interest to ascertain the truth, there is, in this case, no possible material way for the truth to be known with absolute certainty. In the end, however, I believe it isn't the truthfulness or untruthfulness of this claim that is here most germane. It is rather the beautiful illustration it presents with regard to the true meaning of Yeshua's once-and-for-all sacrifice, a truth that is still sadly rejected by almost all of my fellow Jews and  billions of unbelieving Gentiles.

> *But Christ came as High Priest of the good things*
> *to come, with the greater and more perfect taber-*
> *nacle not made with hands, that is, not of this*
> *creation. Not with the blood of goats and calves,*
> **but with His own blood He entered the Most**
> **Holy Place once for all,** *having obtained eter-*
> *nal redemption.* (Heb 9:11-12)

Does this Scripture validate the amazing claim?  We will only know for certain when we meet Him face to face in glory. For now, however, I *can* say with certainty that when Yeshua's side was pierced and the blood rushed out—no matter where it ultimately fell, upon the rocks or upon the mercy seat—the Lord God of Israel proclaimed in a remarkable, undeniable way: Not only was He the Great Provider of everything—He also, at that very moment, became the   ultimate *Provision* for all who would believe.

> *Behold! The Lamb of God who takes away the sin of the world!* (John 1:29b)

RRF
Tiberias, Israel
August 21, 2001

# Distribution and Contacts

To order more copies of this book, *The Messianic Seal of the Jerusalem Church,* or *The Children of God* contact:

### *In Israel:*

Immanuel Gift & Book Center
P.O. Box 1693
Tiberias, 14115, Israel
Tel. 972 6 6723620
Fax 972 6 6723195
e-mail: Orders@TheGalileeExperience.com

### *In North America:*

Your Israel Connection
P.O. Box 76060
Colorado Springs, CO 80970-6060
Tel. 1-800-728-1779 or 1-888-639-8530
e-mail:
Resources@yourisraelconnection.org

Galilee of the Nations Judeo-Christian Resources
P.O. Box 510
Hartsville, TN 37074
Tel. 1-888-838-7928
www.TheGalileeExperience.com

For Your Glory, Inc.
P.O. Box 724
Woodland Park CO 80866
(719) 686-5308
www.foryourglory.org

### To Contact the publisher or author:

Olim Publications
P.O. Box 2111
Tiberias, Israel
Phone: 972 6720535
e-mail: olim@kinneret.co.il